A NEW AMERICA

A NEW AMERICA

HOW MUSIC RESHAPED
THE CULTURE AND FUTURE OF A NATION
AND REDEFINED MY LIFE

TOMMY MOTTOLA

CELEBRA
NEW YORK

CELEBRA
Published by Berkley
An imprint of Penguin Random House LLC
375 Hudson Street, New York, New York 10014

Copyright © 2016 by Thomas D. Mottola

LIBRARY OF CONGRESS CATALOGING-IN-PUBLICATION DATA:

Names: Mottola, Tommy, author.
Title: A new America: how music reshaped the culture and future of a nation and redefined my life/Tommy Mottola.
Description: New York : New American Library, 2016.
Identifiers: LCCN 2016022292 | ISBN 9780451467782 | 9780698143302 (ebook)
Subjects: LCSH: Mottola, Tommy. | Sound recording executives and producers—United States—Biography. | Popular music—United States—History and criticism. | Hispanic Americans—Music—History and criticism. | Music—United States—Latin American influences.
Classification: LCC ML429.M787 A3 2016 | DDC 781.64092 [B]—dc23
LC record available at https://lccn.loc.gov/2016022292

First Edition: November 2016

Printed in the United States of America
1   3   5   7   9   10   8   6   4   2

Jacket photograph of live concert night stage with light by ilbusca/Getty Images
Jacket design by Steve Meditz
Book design by Kristin del Rosario

To my wife,

Thalia,

the love and the light of my life

CONTENTS

Contents

A NEW AMERICA

Follow the Music

This book has probably been building inside me ever since I was stopped cold at the age of three by the music of Tito Puente coming from radios on the streets of the Bronx.

But it wasn't until a few decades later that I really started to pay attention to the unfolding story that's at the heart of *A New America*—and the basis for *The Latin Explosion*, the HBO documentary that I produced in 2015. The turning point in my awareness came in the wake of a conversation with Gloria Estefan that took place back in 1992, about four years after I took over at Sony Music.

"Gloria and I want to talk to you about the next album," her husband, Emilio, had announced on the phone one day in his rich Cuban accent. Without much more of an explanation, he asked me to come to Miami so that we could discuss everything in person.

The Estefans were already family to me—especially after the eventful four years we'd shared since I'd come on board as president at Sony. Prior to that time, my journey in the music industry had taken me from my first career as an artist/musician to learning the ropes of music publishing to making a name for myself as a manager for such acts as Hall and Oates, John Mellencamp, and Carly Simon. As it happened, one of the first pieces of business to cross my desk at Sony had been the pending release of a new Gloria Estefan album. Up until then, Gloria and Emilio and their band had performed and recorded as the Miami Sound Machine. This new release, however, would be the first to feature Gloria's name out front and had the potential, in my view, to truly position her as the next global superstar. But after reviewing the album cover and all the other marketing elements, I came to the conclusion that we needed to develop a much stronger campaign. So I stopped the release in its tracks to revamp everything.

Instead of being upset, Gloria and Emilio were thrilled to have someone at the label who cared and understood what they were all about—and who was willing to reach into the deep pockets of the corporation to boost them to the next level. There may have been some initial resistance at the company to the money I budgeted for marketing the album, but nobody complained when *Cuts Both Ways* went on to exceed everybody's highest hopes—selling many millions of copies worldwide.

Then, in March 1990, while they were on tour for the album, came the terrible accident on a snowy interstate in Pennsylvania when a tractor-trailer plowed into the Estefans' tour bus, hurling

Gloria off a couch inside where she'd been sleeping. After she was lifted out through the smashed windshield, the word was that she might end up a paraplegic. Emilio's first call to me was to say she was going to have surgery the next day. Instead, I was able to get them to hold off so we could locate the leading spine surgeons in New York City and have Gloria flown in on a medevac helicopter. During the four-hour operation that followed, surgeons inserted two eight-inch metal rods inside of her to align and fuse her vertebrae.

The public outpouring of support and prayers was incredible. Gloria's determination throughout the brutal rehabilitation was superhuman. Less than a year after the accident, she returned to the stage at the American Music Awards to sing "Coming Out of the Dark," the first single to be released from her next album, *Into the Light*—which kicked off an enormously successful tour that culminated with her unforgettable performance at the Super Bowl halftime show in Minneapolis.

And that's where we were when Emilio asked me to come to Miami and meet with him and Gloria in person to talk about what was to come next. Here's what I knew: Timing was everything. If ever there was a time to take Gloria completely over the top with her next move, it was right then. She could now release a pop album, attach it to a world tour, and easily double the sales of her last album.

But as I was about to hear loud and clear, Gloria and Emilio wanted to go in another direction. In those days, I spent so much time in Miami that instead of working from a hotel I actually rented a house on Star Island that belonged to the Estefans—whose main residence was nearby. To give you an idea of how close we were, later on I even built my own home next to theirs, which would be paradise found for me; that is, until I was no longer spending as much time in Miami and subsequently sold it to P. Diddy.

In the meantime, there I am in the backyard of this rented house on Star Island, having just arrived from New York and taking a few minutes to enjoy the lush tropical setting with a view of the bay and the Miami skyline beyond, when Emilio stops by to broach the subject of this new album. It's what they've wanted to do for a while—an all-Spanish album release that honored their Cuban roots.

Now, of course, I got it. But anybody with experience in the industry would see how risky that could be. An unexpected turn could cut Gloria's audience in half at precisely the time we were hoping to double it. Besides, Sony had never released a foreign-language album the way you would a pop album. On top of that, I knew just how many walls had to be smashed down to make an all-Spanish album successful. The only way to do it—and not have extreme pushback at Sony—would be to release it *after* the next pop blockbuster album.

And that's what I say to Emilio, telling him, "Listen, it's a great idea. We'll make that album soon. But you have to get her to make another pop album *first*." Then I point out how we've been rolling off these monster Top 40 hits. "Emilio, it makes no sense to stop that momentum and drop a Spanish album now. We can do one and we should, but not as the very next album."

Emilio shrugs and says, "You don't understand. This is more

important to her than anything right now in her life." Then, almost nervously, he adds that Gloria wants to speak with me alone.

This was very rare. Emilio always handled the business side of things.

"Sure," I said. "Lemme talk to her. She doesn't get it."

That's me—no, not Latino but third-generation Italian *and* from the Bronx, where I was raised not to mince words or go against what I know is the right thing to do, in principle or in practice.

Even so, I'm not prepared for the steely conviction I see in Gloria when, a short time later, the two of us sit down in this same backyard of their house I'm renting on Star Island. As close as we've become by this point, I've never seen her act or react like this—with an expression on her face and a tone as serious as someone walking into a court of law.

Everything is quiet. There are none of the usual tropical breezes blowing, no sounds of insects or birds or even of the ocean next to us. Before I can begin, Gloria opens the discussion, laying out her case.

"Doing an album in all Spanish is everything to me, and I know in my heart and in my soul it's what I have to do now. This music is where I come from—my roots, my Cuban roots. I have to go back to that. I can't go forward unless I do this first. This is in my blood. This is me. This says everything about what I am and who I am . . ."

Maybe, I think, this is the direction that has always been inside her. Or maybe this is a priority that's surfaced during the grueling rehab. Whatever it is, I continue to listen as she draws from every emotion, accessing the experience of leaving Cuba at two years old and recalling her father's return to fight during the Bay of Pigs invasion, along with many of Emilio's experiences too.

Gloria stays laser focused on my eyes as she describes the importance of honoring not only her musical roots and the heroes who influenced her as an artist but her relatives and other Cubans, those who left and those who didn't. She goes on and on, laying out her case with power and passion, until finally she stops talking.

"Okay, are you done?" I ask.

"Yes."

"Okay," I say. "So then let's do it."

That moment was a turning point for both of us. Gloria had been so convincing that she disarmed me. No easy feat. She reminded me, above all, that she was the artist and that my job, ultimately, was to be the conduit for what the artist wanted to put out to the world. Yes, I could help guide and direct it, as I'd done my whole career. But at the end of the day the artist is the artist, and I respect the artist more than anything. And she gave me probably the most persuasive and compelling argument that I'd ever heard.

So when I looked her in the eye and said we would do it, that I believed in her and that I believed in her album, my next statement was "Let's go. We'll roll it out and we'll go all the way. And I'm with you a thousand percent. Nothing will stop us."

That was it. We stood up and embraced and then went to work. The album, brilliantly conceived and delivered by Gloria and Emilio, was called *Mi Tierra*—*My Homeland*—and used original songs that called up the classic Cuban traditions of *bolero*, *son*, and *dan-*

zón. Legendary musicians were summoned for the album. From composer and bassist Cachao López, the inventor of the mambo, to jazz trumpeter Arturo Sandoval, to the London Symphony Orchestra, to the immortal Tito Puente on conga and timbales.

It was an amazing album, a groundbreaking work of art, and one I knew would be successful. But I never thought we would go on to sell nine million copies—a huge hit in every country of the world. *Mi Tierra* made music history as the highest-selling Spanish-language album ever released. *Billboard* had to create a whole new way of tracking Latin albums because *Mi Tierra* stayed in that record-breaking number one spot for fifty-eight weeks!

None of that could have been predicted in the immediate aftermath of our talk that day when Gloria sat down to meet with me and explain what was in her heart to do. But soon afterward I began to see the bigger picture—that by doing this album we were building a cornerstone, not only in her career and in her life, but, in fact, in the world of Latinos and Latin music. *Mi Tierra* was that cornerstone to the platform for everything that came after it in the way of Spanish-language music and for all other Latino artists. Even today, it is still regarded as the Holy Grail by everyone who was part of the musical Latin Explosion that happened next.

The bigger picture I'm talking about is what ultimately inspired this book. And yet it was almost twenty years later when the story I wanted to tell finally crystallized for me—on a night in November 2012 as the presidential election returns were playing out on TV and my daughter Sabrina, then five years old, asked me a simple question: "*Papi*, will President Obama win?"

My wife, Thalia Sodi, who was born and raised in Mexico City, sat beside me holding our son, five-month-old Matthew, and she echoed the question in Spanish. When we first met—after being introduced by none other than Gloria and Emilio—Thalia, already a Mexican telenovela star and famous recording artist, was on her way to becoming an extraordinarily successful entrepreneur. In the early days of our courtship, Thalia didn't speak much English and my Spanish was limited. We pushed through our language barrier and were now raising our kids in a bilingual household.

In any language, the answer to Sabrina's question as to who was going to win the presidency came down to the graphic map on the screen. The blue states were Obama's and the red states were for Romney. But the determining factor in who would win? The answer that I kept hearing commentators say over and over came down to one single phrase: *the Latino vote.*

All along I had seen and felt the power of this movement as it built. At Sony, I was there as it came to the fore when we propelled the Latin Explosion, launching the careers of such music icons as Ricky Martin, Jennifer Lopez, Marc Anthony, and Shakira—and, in turn, sending tremors of change into every aspect of the entertainment world and contemporary American culture.

Still, it's hard to convey how stunning it was for me to witness the result of the presidential election and how it put into perspective what the power of Latinos had already become, and would continue to become. Back when I was growing up in the Bronx, Latinos were 1 percent of the US population. Now it was predicted that by 2040 they would be the largest percentage of any population group. And on a night in November 2012, Latinos reelected President Obama with 71 percent of their vote. It dawned on me then that my two youngest children would one day become part of that same Latino voting bloc that is going to influence every presidential election to come. Within my lifetime I had witnessed a shift that was going to be even more powerful than that of the baby boomers.

Next stop? *La Casablanca*, baby!

This is, after all, the unvarnished promise of the American dream. You know that those same people who are now the backbone of the workforce today—whether it's in construction, hotel and restaurant work, landscaping, all the various odd jobs that not a lot of people want to do—will be the doctors, lawyers, and leading professionals of tomorrow. And sooner rather than later, maybe much sooner, we will absolutely have a Latino president.

As Latinos grow in number and continue to move on up, we as a country are the beneficiaries. In all their diversity, they share the richness of their culture in every arena, their sense of pride, their love of family, their respect for heritage and roots, their passion, joy, food, and faith—all the things they do here for America that only strengthen and enrich us all.

A New America celebrates those contributions and marks the major milestones—musical and otherwise—that I hope will speak to our collective journey as the multicultural country we are. It's true that I'm not a historian, and I don't want to claim to be one, but I believe passionately that the trajectory of Latinos, right now, is one of the most significant unfolding stories of our time.

Incidentally, I am aware that there is an ongoing controversy about whether the terms "Latino," "Hispanic," and "Latin" can or should be used for different reasons or interchangeably to refer to people who self-identify as Spanish speakers or as their descendants or who come from countries/backgrounds once colonized by Spain (or one of its neighbors) or who are from indigenous lineages that were under Spanish-speaking control. Certainly, everyone can self-identify by where they or their parents and grandparents were from—Mexican, Puerto Rican, Cuban, and so on. So, for simplicity's sake, I opt to use "Latino" rather than "Hispanic." As my wife points out, "Hispanic" should really refer to anyone from Hispaniola, the island that is home to Haiti and the Dominican Republic.

Besides, "Hispanic," to me, is a gringo term, just kind of homogenized. It's totally gringo. Like Taco Bell. No offense. "Latin" isn't much better. You can call music or food "Latin," which is short for "Latin American," but when you use it to refer to people, it's kind of sanitized too, in my opinion. But "Latino" and "Latina" are not gringo terms, even if they don't really refer to anyone outside of the United States. So there you go.

My point is that Latinos are now the most important, powerful demographic in this country. And for our future they offer the most important and powerful voice of our time. As consumers, Latinos represent more than 1.5 trillion dollars' annual spending, which by itself would constitute the sixteenth largest economy in the world. Over the last several years, Latino businesses have jumped by an astonishing 43 percent. This economic influence alone is a force of nature—one that we ignore only at our peril.

In proclaiming this phenomenon and honoring those who have broken countless barriers in the process, I have chosen to follow the music—as Gloria Estefan sings in "Mi Tierra," the title song from her album that tells the story of a man longing for his "beautiful homeland," his "saintly homeland," who finds his way back to where he comes from and to who he is by following the music.

There is no question but that the surge in the cultural dominance of Latinos in the United States is directly linked to the music and entertainment industries, along with accomplishments in a range of other areas. What music and entertainment did, more than anything, was not only to create opportunities for Latinos but also to garner greater recognition of them in the mainstream.

Just think about the fact that in 1951—when *I Love Lucy* made its debut and Desi Arnaz first sang out his clarion call of *"Babalú!"*—there were fewer than 4 million Latinos in America. There will be 150 million by 2040.

That's proof enough for my stance that if we follow the music, the rhythms, the songs, and the stories that opened so many doors for Latinos in the past, we then can see and hear the possibilities of where we're all going.

CHAPTER ONE

Honey, I'm Home!

When I came to America in 1950, you didn't hear of any Latin
artists on any American records. If anybody opened the doors so
that I could do what I'm doing it was Desi Arnaz. And I assure you
that every Latin performer would tell you the same.

—JOSÉ FELICIANO

Music is where I come from. All kinds of music.

In my neighborhood of the Bronx when I was growing up as a
kid in the 1950s, music was everywhere—all around us, in our
home, in nearby households, in the record stores, in shops and
restaurants, in the nightclubs and bars, and on the street. It was
played by everyone who was part of the real melting pot that made
up our working-class borough of New York City. Latin music was
a major chord, without any of us thinking of it as such, and it
became a huge part of the sound track of our lives.

Maybe that's why a touchstone for me has always been that
distant memory of being three years old and walking through the
Grand Concourse in the Bronx—holding my mother's hand—and
being completely captivated by the sound of Tito Puente and his

band being played on a radio somewhere, loud enough for everyone to hear.

Everything about what I heard—the Afro-Cuban rhythm driven by percussion and wailing horns—must have gone straight into my DNA as I stopped and pulled away from my mother so I could listen more closely. The effect was that of thousands of years of drumbeating contained in one amazing rhythm crashing into the curiosity of a child.

As Gloria Estefan has observed, the very first communication that we have as human beings is the drum—as natural as the human heartbeat. So our response to percussion and rhythm is at our most primal level. We don't have to understand it. It either moves us or it doesn't.

At three years old, I was moved forever. Not only because of the music, but also because of the joy that accompanied it. I'll never forget my mother's reaction. Instead of hurrying me along to wherever we were supposed to be, she stopped to watch me absorb it and, with a beautiful smile on her face, started to clap to the music, encouraging me to clap along too. Right then and there, she took my hands and began to dance with me on the street.

This wasn't an isolated incident. Music was a staple in our household. My mother sang, my father played the piano, my uncle played the guitar, and my sisters sang—in harmony. Whenever there were occasions for a get-together, the three things we could count on were lots of family members, lots of food—we're Italian, after all—and music, music, music.

As the youngest of four kids, I especially wanted to be a part of all the music that mattered to my three older sisters—Jean and Joan (twins) and Mary Ann—who used to dance the cha-cha at home in our house, tuning in to radio shows or playing records of the hottest Latin bandleaders, like Xavier Cugat and Perez Prado. My parents, in these same years, used to frequent the Latin Quarter and the Copa and other upscale nightclubs where you could dance and listen to those very bandleaders. Whenever they returned from going out nightclubbing with friends, my parents would usually bring home a photograph of the two of them—all decked out in this upscale, glamorous world. I still own those big black-and-white photos of my father and mother, souvenirs of that period in time when Latin music gained its first foothold in the United States.

The story of how that happened takes us back to 1930—when the population of Latinos in this country was in the vicinity of one million people. Earlier, during World War I, when huge numbers of American men were sent to fight in Europe and industries found themselves with a gaping hole in their workforce, the call had gone south of the border: "Hey, c'mon up! Plenty of work here!" But as soon as the war ended and the soldiers returned, the message to those same Latinos was very different: "Hey, you can't have our jobs. Get out!"

There was nothing new in this country about anti-immigrant resentment or outright xenophobia—hatred, fear, and bigotry toward anything foreign or "other." But what changed, especially as the country sank deeper into the Great Depression, were the measures being taken to keep the others out. For the first time, the government began imposing limits on the number of immigrants allowed in the US. In addition to an official "border control" created by Congress, for the first time the country began to see mass deportations of Mexican-Americans.

We're talking about eighty-five years ago, more or less, in a climate that was far from welcoming to immigrants in any form. And yet, against those odds, one very catchy little tune arrived to stay.

"Maniiiiiiiiiiiiiiiii . . ."

The song was called "El Manisero." "The Peanut Vendor." You may have never heard of it but, trust me, it struck a chord. The song landed on our shores somewhat differently than the majority of Latinos. It didn't come looking for work. And it wasn't running from political turmoil. It reached America because an American heard it in Cuba, and once it was brought here suddenly it spread like crazy because of what I consider to be the essential ingredients of Latin music—infectious rhythms, and a feeling that is pure *sexy* and, above all, danceable.

When Don Azpiazu and His Havana Casino Orchestra brought the song to a nightclub in New York City, his version would be credited with igniting the rumba dance craze; and seventy years later his recording would be voted into the Latin Grammy Hall of Fame. For good reason. After RCA Victor made a deal to release Azpiazu's 78 rpm single, "El Manisero" went on to become the first Latin record to sell a million copies. It was a pivotal moment that brought together a Spanish song and an American label—complete with the iconic RCA Victor dog staring at the gramophone on the center of the record.

The song needed an American company for a crossover to mainstream consumers. Given the sparse population of Latinos in the early 1930s, this was a market that had little commercial influence. What's more, the numbers were separated by geography—with mostly Puerto Ricans on the East Coast and Mexicans in the Southwest and West. Again, in these days Latinos were not yet called "Latinos" and the process of self-identifying based on national heritage was common. Needless to say, this was a disparate group without the economic power that would happen eight decades later when multiple generations of Americans from twenty-three Spanish- and Portuguese-speaking countries in the Caribbean and Central and South America would be united in a broad demographic bloc.

So it was up to American record companies, movie studios, and even American musicians and actors to bring a song in Spanish to the American public.

Groucho Marx whistled "The Peanut Vendor" in the movie *Duck Soup*. Cary Grant sang it in *Only Angels Have Wings*. Louis Armstrong performed it in English *and* scat; only a few years later Louis' trumpet introduced much of America to "La Cucaracha"— the Mexican song about the cockroach that has lost one of its legs and is trying to walk on the other five.

The Latin music ripple effect had begun, ready for a larger-than-life persona by the name of Xavier Cugat to turn it into a wave. Before he even took up residence as the bandleader of the club at the Waldorf-Astoria—where he reigned for seventeen years—Cugat had become a musical movie star right around the same time that the silent screen was being replaced by the talkies. Flamboyant to the hilt, Xavier Cugat was a character the camera loved. Dressed for a bullfight while holding his baton in one hand and his pet Chihuahua in the other, he brought signature style to everything he did. At the Waldorf, he was a celebrity from the start, setting the bar for all the other nightclubs to try to catch up.

More than that, as a leading figure who served as a bridge between Latin music and mainstream American music, he would have a tremendous impact on the many Latino musicians and artists he influenced. Part of his ability to do all that had to do with his own story and the fact that he, himself, came to the US via a bridge: Cuba.

Born in Spain in 1900, Xavier was a boy when his family relocated to Havana—after his father had problems with the Spanish political regime at the time. In Cuba, Xavier began studying the violin, soon mastering his art by practicing nine hours a day. As fate would have it, he was chosen to perform as first violinist at a concert in Havana along with the famed Italian tenor Enrico Caruso—who was so impressed that he offered to introduce Xavier to the right people in America. Based on that offer, the twenty-one-year-old Cugat and his family made the move to the United States, only to learn a short while later that Caruso had died. That left Xavier Cugat to figure out how to survive on his own—which led to his distinctive look and style that called to Hollywood.

Why the change in the game plan? Well, as Cugat later put it, he'd rather play the Chiquita Banana jingle and have a swimming pool in Beverly Hills than play Bach and starve.

As a nightclub bandleader and recording artist, Cugat studied trends carefully, and became a master at fusing Latin music with the culture and customs of his growing American audience. For example, on the screen or in the club, he'd always make sure to position beautiful Latina dancers doing the steps to the rumba, the cha-cha, or the mambo right next to his musicians, so that anyone could follow the moves and make them their own. He might release an album that called attention to the Mexican hit "Bésame Mucho" or bring Latin flavor to a non-Latin song like "Begin the Beguine." Frank Sinatra sang to Cugat's Latin rhythm when they recorded "Stars in Your Eyes," and Cugat had fun mixing the cultures in pieces like "She's a Bombshell from Brooklyn (and Not from Brazil)."

Much of what I knew of Xavier Cugat and the era he ushered in of upscale nightclub crowds in white tails and furs—which were still going strong in the 1950s—came from my parents' accounts. Later on, however, in the sixties and seventies, Cugat became very familiar to me and known to most of the world because of his wife, Charo, the singer and hugely talented classical guitarist from Spain who had been trained by the legendary Andres Segovia, and who was a character in her own right. How could anyone miss Charo? With the big tits and her "cuchi, cuchi" and an accent you needed subtitles to follow even when she was speaking English, she was almost a comedy act, setting up the Latina bimbo archetype—one that would not do too badly later on for Sofía Vergara, currently the highest-paid female in television.

Remarkably, Xavier Cugat left his stamp on every aspect of the entertainment industry, and he did it across seven decades. But I think his most significant contribution was how he used his own success to fuel the success of other Latino bandleaders, musicians, and performers. None more so than one struggling Cuban immigrant who, more than anyone else, would change the way Latinos were perceived across the country, taking them from immigrants and outsiders to family members who belonged. That historic transformation would be trumpeted by just three words that still reverberate.

"Honey, I'm hoooooome."

For me to truly set the stage that made the ascent of Desi Arnaz both possible and still improbable, I have to describe some of the crosscurrents that play into our larger story. None of this, by the way, was on my radar when I was growing up in the Bronx and falling in love with Latin music by osmosis. Not only that, but in my family and neighborhood—at least the way that I was raised—differences weren't seen as a threat.

But that wasn't the case in lots of places in the country—although only in looking back have I come to recognize the extent of the overt discrimination and the obstacles that towered in front of most Latinos. One of the most dramatic and visual examples of what it was like for a brown-skinned person in the 1930s was captured in a Los Angeles mural entitled *America Tropical*, which was painted by Mexican painter David Alfaro Siqueiros, a contemporary of Diego Rivera. After he was commissioned by a high-society patron to perhaps paint a portrait of happy peasants laboring away, Alfaro used his art for social commentary and portrayed a brown man being crucified by an eagle. Instead of the offended locals addressing the controversy, the mural was promptly whitewashed. As if it had never existed. The commission was canceled and Alfaro was sent back to Mexico. The whitewashing of the concerns of people of color was to be an ongoing issue and outrage.

Prevalent barriers to equal treatment under the law were overt and covert. The signs of Jim Crow, seen in restaurants and other places of business, were overt: "No Dogs, Negroes, or Mexicans." Or the racism could come in institutional forms. Take the fact that even in the early fifties in Texas, American citizens of Mexican descent from families who had been living in the US for many generations were not allowed in the jury box of most counties in the state. What could be more unconstitutional? And that was the question to be posed by a group of sharp Mexican-American lawyers led by Gustavo Garcia and Carlos Cadena—who had been looking for just the right opening to challenge the status quo by filing suit against the state.

It was a case that erupted from a stupid bar fight that would have been forgotten over time had it not managed to land in front of the Supreme Court. As the accounts had it, there were these two guys in a rowdy cantina in Jackson County, Texas, and they got into it about—what else?—women.

One was a migrant field hand with a bum leg by the name of Pete Hernandez. The other, Joe Espinosa, was a tenant farmer. So

Espinosa, full of swagger about how the girls love a real man like him, is giving Hernandez shit about his gimpy leg and how no woman is even going to look at a cripple like him. Hernandez, not taking the comments kindly, goes home, gets a rifle, returns to the cantina, and shoots Espinosa dead.

The jury in Jackson County, Texas, couldn't have been handed a more open-and-shut case. Hernandez was convicted, and normally that would have been the end of it. Except for the fact that Hernandez was an American citizen, and therefore entitled to a fair trial before a jury of his peers. Cadena and Garcia were out to prove that Hernandez couldn't possibly receive a fair trial because he had no Mexican-American peers on the jury. Furthermore, as the lawyers built their argument, they revealed that not a single Mexican-American had been allowed in the jury box of the Jackson County courthouse during the previous twenty-five years.

The suit did not succeed at the state level, but Cadena and Garcia appealed to the US Supreme Court. The significance of this case, *Hernandez v. Texas*, was that it championed the rights of a group of people who were simply struggling *to be seen and to exist*. To the Mexican-American community this was so important that many wanted to be there in person to cheer the lawyers on and hand them whatever little money they could to help with legal expenses. It was the first time that Mexican-American lawyers had ever argued before the highest court in the land.

Of the nine white Supreme Court justices, one of them actually asked Cadena why he referred to his client as a "citizen of Mexican descent." Another judge interrupted to ask, "They call them greasers down there, don't they?"

Its own bias notwithstanding, the Supreme Court returned with a landmark decision that was a victory not only for the lawyers and Hernandez—who was tried again by a jury of his peers and convicted again—but for the legal rights of all Mexican-Americans and other Latino citizens. American justice had prevailed, opening the door to challenges on behalf of anyone made to feel invisible or barred from access—whether it was to bathrooms, water fountains, movie theaters, or jobs.

As an interesting sidenote to everything that was going on in 1954, the year this case came to the Supreme Court, it so happened to be the same year that Sonia Sotomayor was born—to be raised not far from where I was growing up right there in the Bronx.

This is not to say that all the walls were about to start tumbling down. On the contrary, to complicate this great victory, you know what happened a month after that landmark decision? *One* month later?

President Eisenhower launched a campaign to make Mexicans without documents simply vanish. The name of the campaign says it all: Operation Wetback. The focus was on getting rid of the Mexican migrants who'd come to pick grapes, tomatoes, and other crops, along with busboys, factory workers, and occupants of nearly every low-level job that fueled the American economy. The operation was run with jeeps and trucks that communicated with aircraft overhead to round brown people up and take them to detention centers for deportation if they couldn't prove their citizenship. Local police in California offered to help by staging their own raids. Native Americans in Arizona were even offered three dollars for every Mexican they could apprehend. All in all, as many as 1.3 million Mexicans were deported or left the country voluntarily during this period. It's believed that thousands of those forced out may have been *legal* Mexican-Americans.

How do you reconcile those two opposing messages? One month, you're gaining the right to sit in the jury box. The next month you're being hunted and kicked out of the country.

The truth is that sometimes you can't reconcile that kind of painful contradiction that calls into question your very right to belong. At the same time, as history will bear out, if you can be innovative and entrepreneurial, you learn to seek other avenues for belonging.

Take for instance the path forged by a man named Don Prudencio Unanue, an immigrant to the United States, originally from Spain by way of Puerto Rico, who in 1936 bought the business name "Goya" for a buck and began to sell sardines and olives out of a small storefront on Duane Street in Manhattan. Nothing very auspicious. But he had no choice other than to make it work. Unanue was already fifty years old, with a wife and four children to support.

At the start he sold olives and olive oils to fellow Spaniards looking for a taste of their homeland. Soon he expanded to do the same for others among the ever-growing number of immigrants from the Caribbean and Central and South America, who also longed for the flavors of the past. In the postwar years, as newly arrived immigrants gravitated to communities where family members or friends were already settling in, Goya products moved into these pockets, grew with them, and became trusted like family.

Throughout the fifties, during the large migration of Puerto Ricans to the mainland, Goya was there to sell the rice, beans, and spices that the newcomers wanted. In the late fifties and early sixties came the influx of Cubans, and Goya would offer products for their tastes by buying out Cuban companies, diversifying *and* eliminating competition. In later years, Goya did the same in catering to the Dominicans, Colombians, Ecuadorians, and Peruvians. A key to Goya's success was that it hired employees from these same immigrant groups to help develop, test, and refine its products before they hit the shelves. And so whenever new customers went to the market looking for familiar foods and spices, they found the real deal. Plus, Goya wasn't sold through distributors; they sold directly to the stores. Goya knew its customers like few other companies.

What Goya figured out, and what was lost on the big corporations, was the potential buying power of this Latino demographic *and*, most importantly, how to tap it. As Goya would assert, they got to know the tastes of those who lived in the neighborhoods where their products were sold because the people who worked for Goya lived in those same neighborhoods. Goya's growth, clearly, became directly tied to the rise in the Latino population. It sold the beans that *Abuelita* used to soak all night before she seasoned and cooked them. Recognizing that *Abuelita's* daughter might be working long hours out of the house and didn't have the time and inclination to soak those same beans, Goya simply prepared the beans in cans that could be easily heated up by the next generation, yet still to *Abuelita's* taste.

As a visionary entrepreneur, Don Prudencio Unanue created a brand that subtly unified Latinos, who, it's important to note, weren't necessarily drawn together because of similarities in overall culture. On the contrary, these are consumers who are deeply aware and proud of the differences between their countries of origin and don't choose to be lumped in together as all wanting to be seen as the same. These differences become very clear when you understand that today Goya Foods sells roughly forty types of beans because the people from each country or culture tend to prefer a specific type. Which explains the expression about Latinos: "United by language, divided by beans."

Then again, there is nothing ever like good food or good music to bridge an ocean of differences, right? And, indeed, back in the late 1940s—a period in which there were revolutionary innovations in media and in different forms of communication—music would offer an unprecedented opening for Latin culture to begin to translate to the mainstream, thanks to the biggest advance of the time: television.

World War II had stopped the manufacturing of television sets in America so that all equipment and energy could be used for the war effort. That meant that in 1946, after the war was over, there were only some six thousand operating televisions in the country—most of them in New York City. The number grew rapidly. But, still, when Tito Puente and Perez Prado started playing at the Latin

Quarter in the late forties, only 4 percent of homes had primitive black-and-white sets.

Television sales multiplied exponentially in the early fifties, soon covering more than 50 percent of American homes. For the first time in history nearly all eyes could be simultaneously focused on the same people, shows, and events that were produced by only a few networks. This was focus and power on a scale the world had never seen.

No doubt, the stage had been set and was ready for someone to come along and seize this megaplatform—someone who had already walked through doors opened by Xavier Cugat.

As a boy growing up in Santiago, Cuba, Desi Arnaz would have seemed like the last person to need a helping hand from anyone. That may come as a surprise for those who assume that Desi was the destitute immigrant and Lucille was the affluent American. It was quite the opposite.

It was Lucy who came from very humble and difficult circumstances. Born about an hour south of Rochester, she lost her dad when she was two. She was raised in her grandfather's home, which was later lost in an economic tumble. Lucy's childhood left her with an immigrant's frugality. Later, when unused boxes of pencils began disappearing from the workplace of *I Love Lucy* writers, nobody suspected that Lucy, the highest-paid woman on television, was the one bringing them home and stockpiling them in a closet.

Desi, on the other hand, grew up amid great wealth and splendor.

In fact, his maternal grandfather was one of the founders of the Bacardi rum company. The family owned three farms and a beach house—various holdings that came with boats, a stable of horses, maids, and chauffeurs. Desi's father was a beloved mayor of Santiago, popular for revitalizing the city, and was poised to have a promising career as a national representative. But in 1933, when Fulgencio Batista overthrew the regime of Gerardo Machado and rebels swept the country, Desi's father was jailed in Havana. In the chaos, mob rule broke out and the prisons were emptied of inmates—sending murderers, thieves, and rapists to plunder the homes of the wealthier citizens.

Moments before the marauders arrived at Desi's home, a family friend was able to rescue him and his mother and get them to safety. The next day, when mother and son returned, they found the family piano smashed to pieces, their car upside down with its tires gone, and the house's contents scattered. Desi would later describe finding the remnants of the last image he retained of his childhood home: his guitar. It had been set afire and was left outside with the neck "still smoldering."

So Desi made his way to America, along with his family, arriving in Miami as part of one of the first waves of Cubans stripped of familial wealth. But, like many other Cubans who would follow in later waves, he had an entrepreneurial streak that was immediately apparent. While he was still in high school in Miami, Desi helped his dad start a small business importing tiles, and then he persuaded his father to move out of the boardinghouse where they were paying rent and into their small company warehouse. When they discovered that it was infested with rats, they cleared them out with a baseball bat.

Not long after joining his first band as a singer, Desi found a way to boost his band's popularity. He convinced friends to flood the dance floor every time they took the stage, and their response made it appear that he was the hottest guy around. And sure enough, when Xavier Cugat was in Miami auditioning musicians, that was how Desi Arnaz caught his attention.

The bandleader not only auditioned Desi but brought him to New York as a member of his house orchestra. Bam. That was it. During the brief but pivotal mentorship, Cugat handed Desi a blueprint for how to fuse Latin music with the mainstream—how to be authentic and engage the audience at the same time.

This immersion may have prompted Desi to describe Cuban music as the love affair between the African drum and the Spanish guitar, while the horns in his orchestra could take this passion to another level. In any event, when Desi decided to return to Miami and go out on his own, Cugat loaned him the well-known name of his orchestra. Problem was, the Cugat name was all Desi had. There were relatively few Cuban musicians in Miami at the time. Hilariously, Desi was able to assemble a motley crew—an Italian on bass, a Jewish pianist, another Italian on sax, another Jew on violin, and there *was* a Spanish drummer. Unfortunately, they didn't play Cuban music, other than "The Peanut Vendor."

Their opening set on the first night of their next engagement was ostensibly a disaster. But before they were given the boot, Desi decided to improvise on the spot. His idea, he would later admit, came from his childhood in Cuba and seeing people on the streets during carnivals banging on conga drums and turning frying pans and spoons into a party.

His band that night couldn't have been further removed from those memories. So he went backstage with a bottle of Bacardi and told his orchestra to drink up—quick! As soon as the next set began, he hit the conga drum, got the pianist to join in by playing chords to the same beat, and handed the violinist a frying pan and two spoons. From there, he slung the conga drum over his shoulder with a leather strap and started to dance to the beat. As the night wore on, he kept it up, to the point that everybody in the club was following Desi around the dance floor. Desi claimed that was the night the conga line arrived in America.

Not many years later, after he had made the leap from successful bandleader to performer on Broadway and in the movies, you can only wonder what Lucy was thinking when she first met Desi on the movie set of *Too Many Girls*. Lucy was five years older than Desi, and trying to corral a man with a voracious appetite who appealed to so many women was a difficult and endless task. Lucy often cracked that *Too Many Girls* was really the story of his life.

You could say that the same entrepreneurial spirit that brought the first conga line to America was also behind the creation of *I Love Lucy*. When CBS first asked Lucy to convert her radio show, *My Favorite Husband*, into a TV sitcom, she was all for it, but she wanted Desi to play the role of her TV husband. That was a problem. Lucy's "husband" on the radio show was an all-American bank vice president. Desi's accent locked him out of that, and besides, CBS executives just couldn't fathom their audience accepting an all-American redhead married to a Cuban with a conga drum.

But Desi returned to the same operating principle that set off the first conga line: *There must be a way.* He sketched out an act with a friend and refined it with Lucy on a brief stage tour. CBS execs sold the concept to a sponsor, Philip Morris, in less than forty-eight hours. But other obstacles remained.

The execs wanted the show broadcast live in New York like their other shows. The couple wanted to remain at home in California. Desi solved the problem by reinventing television.

Nobody had ever done a situation comedy on film up to that point. When the execs demanded it be shot in front of a live audience to get natural laughter, Desi innovated. He got the idea to stage the show like a play in front of three cameras and a studio audience. That not only meant finding and customizing a studio; it meant inventing all-new lighting schemes. Desi did the impossible by luring in the industry's leading director of photography, a major feat when you consider there was no money in the budget to afford the guy.

Every risk, every decision, every battle paid off. From the moment the show first aired, everyone in America wanted to be home and in front of their TV set on Monday nights to watch Lucille Ball and Desi Arnaz in *I Love Lucy.* That included my parents, my older sisters, and me. My favorite part about the show was watching Ricky Ricardo as a bandleader performing in his nightclub, Babalu. Again, as a little kid in the fifties, I wasn't conscious of it being Latin music, per se. All I knew was that I loved it.

It didn't matter if you were three years old or seventy. You were an *I Love Lucy* fan. Who knew that a simple half-hour sitcom could have such cultural significance?

Think about it. A milk-white redhead from Rochester, New York, married to a brown-skinned bandleader from Cuba with grease in his hair and as thick an accent as you can get. At the time, that was a no-no. But instead of covering it up, they addressed it and turned the taboo into comedy. Eventually, the names Lucille Ball and Desi Arnaz would be a symbol for Latino integration into American culture.

The fact that the two were married gave credence to their show's comical portrait of how this crazy merging of cultures and differences could possibly work. Lucy was a genius. No one comes close, in my view. Once, when asked who should get credit for the great success of the show, Desi replied that he and the crew deserved 10 percent. Ninety percent belonged to Lucy.

The brilliance of Desi was how—even with an accent that turned "explainin'" to "splainin'"—he figured out a way to sidestep the stereotype. Without being heavy-handed or self-conscious, he did it just by playing himself.

Lucie Arnaz, the daughter of Lucille Ball and Desi Arnaz, put it so well when she observed, "To my knowledge, it was the first time that a Latin male was seen by American audiences on television who wasn't depicted as somebody who was lazy, or a worker, or a slime-bag lounge lizard . . . or somebody who was sleeping under a sombrero." When Ricky Ricardo showed up, Lucie asserted, "He was handsome. He was successful. He wasn't a huge star, but he was doing well. He had a good job at a little club. People liked him. He was sexy. He was smart. He was funny. He was married to a beautiful woman. They lived in a nice enough apartment, but he wasn't rich. He was a middle-class American guy, successful like many other middle-class Americans. That was huge for Latinos. Nobody ever talked down to Ricky Ricardo."

And behind the scenes, in their shared work, nobody ever talked down to Desi or Lucy. All creativity was channeled through the two of them. But as Lucie remembers, it was her father who thrived on running production "and picking the scripts and talking to the writers, all the stuff that my mother didn't like doing at all. He did the invisible stuff that nobody saw."

In his quest to do things according to his vision, Desi was known for not giving in, even fighting all the way up to the top of Philip Morris, where the chairman of the board once backed him with an interoffice memo that read: "To whom it may concern. Don't fuck around with the Cuban."

By the end of the six-year run of the show, Desi and Lucy's production company had grown to be able to produce hundreds of hours of programming on various shows, and it purchased RKO Studios, giving it thirty-five stages and the biggest motion picture and television facility in the world.

Their marriage was strained by work obligations and Desi's infidelities from the start. They fought and grew apart, but still came together to transform modern entertainment forever.

I Love Lucy produced ratings that nobody will ever see again. *Nobody.* The episode in the second season where Lucy and Ricky have a son was, at that point, the top-rated show of all time. It aired on the day before Dwight Eisenhower's presidential inauguration in 1953, and the audience for that show went *over and beyond that of the inauguration* by two million viewers. Half of all the television sets in America routinely tuned in to *Lucy.* Some nights, the proportion exceeded seven out of ten.

In all this time since, from 1957 when its sixth and last season aired, *I Love Lucy* has been viewed continuously. It's *never* been off the air. In survey after survey, it has been repeatedly voted the greatest TV show of all time. And through all the sociological changes, it's found a continued relevance for generation after generation.

Years after *I Love Lucy* had moved on to rerun heaven, where it will exist in perpetuity, people would come over to Desi Arnaz wherever he happened to be and greet him by saying, "Honey, I'm home."

No matter how often that happened, he'd always go out of his way to respond warmly. And that makes sense, especially when you think about those three words as a form of gratitude for the opportunity and the home that the United States had given him, and hopefully will continue to give fellow immigrants from the Caribbean and Central and South America . . . and from everywhere else in the world.

CHAPTER TWO

I Like to Be in America

It's an amazing thing when a young girl comes up to you with tears in their eyes . . . and then they burst out with, "You make me feel like I can do anything in the world." And I'm thinking, "I know exactly how you feel because that's what Rita Moreno did for me." Just seeing Rita in *West Side Story*, just that one movie, that one person and that one role, inspired me to go and do all the things that I've been able to accomplish. Rita Moreno allows this little Puerto Rican girl from the Bronx to sit here in awe and wonder at what has happened to my life.

—JENNIFER LOPEZ

Any kid who laughed at *I Love Lucy* in my Bronx neighborhood in the fifties walked out the door the next morning and faced the reality that there were certain lines not to be crossed. Didn't matter if you were Italian, Puerto Rican, black, Jewish, Irish, white, or mixed. Crossing those lines could put you in the wrong neighborhood and was an invitation to an ass kicking (if you were lucky) or worse (if you weren't).

We all embraced *I Love Lucy*. But we all understood the ground rules of *West Side Story*.

As a modernized musical based on *Romeo and Juliet*, Shakespeare's tragic drama of star-crossed lovers who defy the dividing lines between their families, *West Side Story*—a 1950s Broadway smash—was more than a timeless tale brilliantly told. By showing what happens when a Latina named Maria and an American guy named Tony fall in love and have to pay the consequences of crossing the forbidden line, *West Side Story* could not have been more relevant to the times.

Remember, the show was not a period piece in 1957 when the original Broadway production premiered. With music by Leonard Bernstein, lyrics by Stephen Sondheim, and book by Arthur Laurents, it had iconic staging and choreography by Jerome Robbins—who, along with Robert Wise, codirected the 1961 movie version of *West Side Story*. Both the stage musical and the film were groundbreaking in so many ways, as anyone in show business can attest. Most people today are not aware, however, that in the movie almost none of the actors who played the Puerto Rican characters were Latino.

There was one exception: Rita Moreno.

She didn't just have the good fortune to be cast in the movie's plum role of Anita, which would earn her one of the eleven Academy Award nominations received by *West Side Story*. Rita crossed every possible line on her way to the evening of the Oscar awards ceremony in 1962—where she nervously waited as Rock Hudson opened the envelope to announce the winner of her category.

As the story goes, it was late in the night and at that point *West Side Story* had swept every award it had been nominated for, and Rita was convinced, "My Puerto Rican luck—I'll be the only one who doesn't get an award."

So what happened? Well, in order for you to appreciate the

answer, I have to give some context for just how momentous this was and how other Latino celebrities were making it by crossing their own lines in the 1950s and '60s.

Tito vs. Tito.

That was how the battle of the bands between Tito Puente and Tito Rodriguez—one of the fiercest, most exciting mambo rivalries that kept on going throughout the fifties—was promoted at the landmark venue at Fifty-third Street and Broadway in New York, the Palladium.

There was Tito Puente out in front of his orchestra, hurling his sticks against his paired cylindrical drums—the timbales. And there was Tito Rodriguez, a singer and bandleader known by the nickname that came from one of his songs: *el Inolvidable*. The unforgettable one.

Billboards advertising each of the two were placed on either side of the street. Audiences packed the dance floor and grouped together like fans at a sporting event to cheer on their favorite. There was space for a thousand dancers on the ballroom floor, and the two bandleaders battled each other in every musical way, with Puente once bringing in a fourth trumpet to send a message to the three in Rodriguez's orchestra. And Rodriguez coming back at Puente with songs like "Avísale a Mi Contrario (Que Aquí Estoy Yo!)"—or "Tell My Opposition I Am Here!"—as well as "Que Pena Me Da," translated: "I Pity You."

Everybody who heard the mambo went so crazy and lost all

their inhibitions on the dance floor that the mambo must have been some kind of wild aphrodisiac! You're talking about this syncopated Afro-Cuban mambo rhythm that bass player and bandleader Cachao López has been credited with inventing and that his countryman Perez Prado, one of my favorite Latin musicians, went on to refine as the King of the Mambo, turning it into the dance craze it was. Tito Puente, born in Harlem to Puerto Rican parents, and Tito Rodriguez, who came to New York from Puerto Rico, fanned the already hot mambo flames by bringing in the latest jazz influences they were hearing played at the one and only Birdland—the club where you'd go to hear Charlie Parker, Lester Young, and all the other top black jazz names of the time.

In effect, this fusion between Latin music and Afro-American jazz was served up to desegregate the nightclub world at the Palladium, where Latinos and whites and blacks and all ethnicities were together not only in the orchestra but on the dance floor, moving their bodies to the beat with one another in very sexy ways. The rope lines that continued to separate the races in almost every other venue in America were torn down there in New York on that packed dance floor. It didn't matter what ethnicity or color you were, as long as you could move to that dynamic rhythm. Apparently there was one part of the dance floor where only the best dancers gathered. You really had to bring it, and if you didn't have it to bring—you were quickly driven out of that corner.

By doing what they did so well, Tito Puente and Tito Rodriguez, along with the other celebrity bandleaders, blurred the color lines in ways that somewhat paralleled what was happening in those decades in major-league baseball—after Jackie Robinson blazed a trail onto the playing field in 1947. Generally it was still harder for Latinos who wanted to play baseball in the 1950s than it was for arriving musicians. Pockets of opportunity were more numerous for musicians who could choose to live where they wanted. But when baseball players were signed in the Caribbean they were often sent first to minor-league teams in the deep and prejudiced South. There, they were frequently alone without being able to understand the English language, and without having anyone to translate for them. The racism was more pronounced, more overt.

But the baseball diamond was no different than the stage in a significant way. Athletes and musicians were all out in front of the public, and those who excelled and lifted people to their feet became celebrities who were embraced and loved because they showed what was possible, and set up the change to come for everyone else.

Roberto Clemente, from Puerto Rico, had a similar kind of impact in the world of baseball that Desi Arnaz had achieved in popular culture. Latinos would actually stop what they were doing and move close to a radio when someone called out that the great Clemente was coming up to bat. American fans shared the love for Clemente—who became appointment viewing for Pittsburgh Pirates fans and many others just as *I Love Lucy* was for everyone else.

After Clemente made his debut with the Pirates in 1955, he encountered much of the same racial backlash that Jackie Robinson had faced seven years earlier. Black and Latino, Clemente also had a very pronounced accent that turned *V*s into *B*s—which was how he came to be known and made fun of for saying, "Baseball been berry, berry good to me." The more that sportswriters kept trying to change his name into "Bob" or "Bobby," the more Roberto insisted he preferred his given name. When he was the object of racist comments about Latinos, he would address it as a statesman, noting that he didn't see color or think of it as a way to define himself. Sometimes he would also call it out, as he once commented, "Some people act like they think I live in a jungle someplace."

As a trailblazer, Clemente is considered by many baseball buffs to be peerless because he really could do it all: run, field, throw, and hit with power. But what may have distinguished him even more was his belief that achieving success was only an opportunity to do something with it for others. As he put it, "Any time you have an opportunity to make a difference in this world and you don't, then you are wasting your time on earth."

Over the course of his career's almost two decades, Roberto Clemente became the first Latino to win a National League Most Valuable Player Award, the first Latino to become the MVP in the World Series, and the first Latino to enter the Hall of Fame. Tragically, the last honor came way too early. On New Year's Eve of 1972, while he was en route to bring supplies to victims of an earthquake in Nicaragua, the plane he was aboard crashed at sea.

Baseball players are usually measured by statistics. But the success of Clemente goes far beyond the number of home runs he hit or his batting average. Roberto, on top of being a humanitarian who never forgot where he came from, activated an influx of Latino ballplayers from all over the Caribbean. That phenomenon really began to show itself in the sixties, and has continued ever since.

Today, when you look at the possibilities for a person wanting to break into the arenas of sports and Latin music, it can be assumed that being Latino would not be much of a deterrent. But for those trying to break into fields like film and television, especially in the forties and fifties, Latino talent wasn't what the studios or networks were calling for. Or at least, that's how many actors and actresses with Latino-sounding names must have felt in trying to navigate across difficult lines.

When you hear the name Rita Hayworth, it conjures the image of a red-haired movie star and classic American pinup of the forties. You might be surprised, as I was, that she was in fact born Margarita Carmen Cansino. Hayworth changed her name and her look to get her break. Raquel Welch came into the world as Jo Raquel Tejada—her father was an aeronautical engineer who'd been born in Bolivia. Sammy Davis Jr. was part Cuban. One of the most ironic cases of misunderstood identity has to be that of the second Latino (after José Ferrer) to ever win an Academy Award—Anthony Quinn. Born in Mexico as Antonio Rodolfo Quinn Oaxaca and raised in Los Angeles, Quinn proudly went out of his way to let people know of his Mexican heritage. But it didn't matter, because most people thought he was Greek after his starring turn in the film *Zorba the Greek*. He won his Academy Award for Best Supporting Actor for his role in *Viva Zapata!* I guess the voters that year thought he was *acting* like a Mexican.

Granted, a name change alone would not have guaranteed success to a talented young Latina who was looking to break into show business in the 1940s and '50s. So what do you do? If you're Rita

Moreno, you cross the line and find your way on your own so others can follow. As she put it, "It's so interesting to have become a role model when I didn't have one myself. But back then there was nobody. Nooooooobody that I could look up to who was a Latina in the English-speaking world."

In the late fifties, when *West Side Story* was all the talk of Broadway, my parents didn't take me to see it. We went to see lots of other musicals but I was too young, in their view, for *West Side Story*, what with its gang violence and tragic ending. They eventually relented, once I was an adolescent, so I did get to see the movie and it was incredible. Up until then, I had never seen anything that addressed social issues in such an entertaining, dramatic form, certainly not like that movie. And because of the fact that our changing neighborhood did have those lines between gangs who were Italian, Irish, Puerto Rican and so on, *West Side Story* offered a moral—as a cautionary tale for me to avoid being drawn into situations that would involve warring factions.

Fortunately, with credit due to my family, who watched over me like hawks and kept me rooted, I stayed out of the fray. That solid upbringing kept me grounded in many other ways too. Even as a teen, I definitely saw the impact that the movie of *West Side Story* had on audiences at the time. Later on, I would be able to understand more deeply what Rita Moreno meant to the Latino community and to the culture. From that I developed enormous admiration for how she changed the lives of everybody who aspired to make it in show business as an outsider, simply showing others, *This is possible.*

Her story was not particularly dramatic from the start. Rita often recalled how much she loved her first five years of life in Puerto Rico in the 1930s, a life that was free of dividing lines. The people she encountered in her daily routine had a variety of skin tones. As far as Rita could tell, nobody with one skin color was treated any differently than anyone with another.

There was no great upheaval to push her to America. No political revolution, no desperate need for work. Her mother wanted to get away from Rita's father. The drama began once they'd boarded the SS *Carabobo*. A nightmare storm hit and waves sent every passenger running for the toilets, and the toilets were soon overflowing down the deck with every form of bodily discharge. It was like that for five unrelenting days before the ship reached the Statue of Liberty. I guess that was their welcome to the immigrant's America: dealing with the shit, alongside the promise of better to come.

Rita stepped straight into the stereotype: a walk-up apartment in the Bronx packed with three families of relatives, the rumble of the elevated train, the roaches, soot, and bedbugs, the landlord cutting off the heat at night, and a strange language she couldn't comprehend that was coming from the other side of the new dividing line. She experienced it all at school: blond-haired white girls on one side, and her, dark haired and light skinned but still called "dirty," on the other.

These days, any child just about anywhere with a gifted voice and natural beauty would be directed to a variety of programs in the performing arts. Rita's performances early on were limited to being played out on the rooftop of the apartment building her mother moved them into in Washington Heights. Options did open up for singing and dancing at local parties and events while she dodged bullies in the wrong neighborhoods and sprinted home a few steps ahead of the word "spic." She ran with her front-door key clenched between her knuckles to defend herself in case she couldn't get it in the lock fast enough. Rita was living a version of *West Side Story* long before she ever got the call to act in it.

It was no straight shot from that childhood rooftop to the rooftop dance scene that played out to the song "America" in *West Side Story* and blew the public away. The lines standing in her way to break into Hollywood were more insidious, even invisible. The good news was that Rita's beauty got her enough notice to be described as a Latina Elizabeth Taylor and before long an interview with Louis B. Mayer, plus a contract with MGM. The bad news? She was typecast as the generic barefoot sexpot in various exotic settings. The native Tahitian girl in *Pagan Love Song*. The Amazonian girl in *Jivaro*. She invented what she called "the universal ethnic accent" to cover the voice of any Latina, Polynesian, Arab, Native American, or slave girl—all the while hoping to one day get a script that spoke to her soul.

Then one day there was no more invisible line. She was simply invisible, dropped from her contract.

Fortunately, a photo of Rita caught the attention of editors at *Life* magazine, who put her on the cover, ultimately leading to an audition and the role of Anita in the movie version of *West Side Story*. Obviously, this was the break she had been waiting for. But when she began to prepare for the part, she was seriously conflicted about one of the lines in the song "America," which was, *"Puerto Rico, you ugly island. Island of tropic diseases."*

When she first heard it, Rita later confessed, she was offended, pointing out, "Of all the reasons not to like Puerto Rico—tropic diseases? In fact they hardly exist there." After hearing that the part was hers she was in the middle of celebrating when she thought, "Oh my God, that line. I can't sing that. I can't do that to my people."

Luckily, the filmmakers decided to change the lyric to: *"Puerto Rico, my heart's devotion,"* sung sarcastically, *"let it sink back in the ocean."* It wasn't perfect but for Rita it was a happy day when she didn't have to sing *"island of tropic diseases."*

In other respects, Stephen Sondheim's lyrics to "America" are genius and at the heart of the immigrant story and struggle. The women's chorus says it all: *"I like to be in America! Okay by me in America! Ev'rything free in America. For a small fee in America!"*

Everything about the filmmaking that went into *West Side Story* was genius. It was one of those rare movies that was so timely, touching a nerve that connected mainstream viewers to the Latino experience of the day, but it was also timeless—a movie that would remain in the public consciousness forever. As Rita Moreno would say, "It wasn't your average great movie; it was your unbelievably unique great movie."

The role of Anita, a bombshell spitfire, was one of those once-in-a-lifetime roles that Rita brought to life so definitively she would spend the next seven years turning down roles that would have sent her back to playing the generic barefoot exotic lovely or pigeonholed her into playing only bombshell spitfires. The truth is that Rita's performance brought so much more to the role of Anita. She channeled the experience of Latina immigrants. The humor needed to survive struggle, the passion and faith to overcome. The courage to stand up for yourself and the people you love while being caught in the cross fire. The strength to confront senseless hatred. And gratitude for opportunities that only appear after long periods of grit and determination.

And there she was on Oscar night in 1962, as *West Side Story* was called, award after award, for nine of its eleven nominations, and with only two remaining, Rita was convinced that she would be the one nominee from the film not to go home with an Oscar. Judging by the surprised look on Rock Hudson's face after naming the different nominees (one of whom was Judy Garland) for Best Actress in a Supporting Role, and then opening the envelope, you might have been led to conclude that Rita was not a shoo-in. But sure enough, as soon as he read the name, "Rita Moreno," no one could miss the shock and relief on her face, and how she had to compose herself to stop from running to the stage. Her Puerto Rican luck worked in her favor. *West Side Story* won ten of its eleven nominations, leaving it to someone else to go home empty-handed.

It was just such a great moment for the world to witness. She was the first Latina to win an Academy Award, and the only actual Puerto Rican in a movie that dealt with an immigrant group of Latinos in America, and there she was—being handed her award by a very happy Rock Hudson, a white, gay male who clearly dealt with dividing lines of his own.

Famously, when Rita stood at the podium to accept her award, all she could muster was: "I can't believe it. Good Lord!" A pause followed. And then, "I leave you with that."

As soon as she walked off the stage, she was already remorseful that she hadn't been able to say more. It weighed on her for a long time until she heard a story about what that moment had meant, speech or not, as she remembered hearing it:

> Liz Torres, this wonderful comedienne who lived in El Barrio in New York at the time, said that it was very hot on Oscar night; all the windows were open and as she says, the Barrio is a very noisy place. We're noisy people. We laugh loud; we cry loud; everything is loud, loud. And she said you could hear all the TV sets coming out of the windows in this huge neighborhood. And when Rock Hudson came up to name the nominees for the best supporting actress, the whole neighborhood became absolutely dead silent. And when my name was mentioned as the winner, she said that neighborhood went truly crazy. Yelling and screaming in Spanish out the windows. "She did it!" And people were crying and laughing and yelling. When Liz told me that story, I just burst into tears.

Rita Moreno is a national treasure, a triple threat, and a powerhouse, and one of the few entertainers to win not only an Oscar, but an Emmy, a Tony, and a Grammy. She went on to perform at Bill Clinton's presidential inauguration in 1993. Another president, George W. Bush, would drape the Medal of Freedom around her neck.

What's amazing about Rita is that even at the age of eighty-four plus, after a forty-five-year marriage, after watching her daughter grow to raise her two grandsons, she is still focused on doing more to remove the lines that divide and to make sure that those who are here have the opportunity to truly say, "I like to be in America."

She once described the tension between Americans and Latinos as a push and pull. "Americans love our food," Rita acknowledged. "They adore our food. They love the music because it makes 'em bounce. They love what the music does to them. It's not only energetic; it's joyous and sexy too." But, as she went on to say, "They fear what they love about us. They fear our sexuality. They fear our passion because we are people who are not embarrassed to weep or yell with anger. . . . We're very passionate people. We tend to be loud. It's part of our heritage. When I performed in Puerto Rico, the people were not just applauding; they were yelling and carrying on. All of those things are charming from a distance. But the Americans don't want to get too close to it."

She has a point. And that push and pull, as Rita calls it, showed up in surprising ways in the musical, cultural revolution that came out of the 1950s and burst into the '60s, just like *West Side Story*.

CHAPTER THREE

La Bamba

People always go to the hippest thing. The thing that really speaks to them, whether they understand it or not. Even if they didn't understand the words, "La Bamba" was great to them.

—CHEECH MARIN

If you were to ask anyone who knew me back in my high school history class, they would probably be surprised by my later interest in the sweeping historical changes that took place around us during our formative years. Back then, I couldn't wait for the final bell to throw off my jacket and tie, get behind the wheel of my turquoise GTO, and leave skid marks on the pavement.

Hey, what sixteen- or seventeen-year-old in the 1960s really wanted to be in school? I'd look for any opportunity to race my car or go to wherever the hot-looking girls were hanging out. Basically what most guys of my generation were into at the time. Other than that, music was becoming even more of a dominant influence in my life—especially as I started to gravitate toward having a career as a singer and musician where my area of expertise would be as a pop and R&B guy.

Along with the Latin music that I followed in my neighborhood, some of the Latino artists I loved had inspired me as a young musician. Back when I learned to play trumpet at eight years old, my first performance was of a piece that had been made famous by Perez Prado. When I switched to guitar in my teens, I used to slap the neck as I played, adding rhythms and chords that had a Latin flavor. But I should also add that I did come of age in the time of rock 'n' roll. And guess what. Unbeknownst to a lot of people, Latinos were some of the original rockers.

Let's look at why that fact is so little known. In the late fifties, a seventeen-year-old singer from California without an accent had a choice. He could be Ricardo Valenzuela. Or he could be Ritchie Valens. Over the radio, how would anybody know? Though his look was clearly Mexican, the record label that was going to put out his first single pushed the name change to make sure that Ritchie was not boxed in by his ethnicity. The thinking made sense, because, hey, once you're in the door . . .

Still, the fact is, Ritchie spoke English at home in the San Fernando Valley, where he was growing up in Los Angeles, not Spanish. And the ballad "Donna" was inspired by Ritchie's real-life high school relationship with a white girl named Donna Ludwig and their breakup after her parents pulled her away. But after Ritchie heeded the advice that listeners could be put off by his Mexican last name, the voice attached to the song gave radio listeners in the heartlands in 1958 no clue that Valens' last name was really Valenzuela.

"Donna" was the A side of the record, released in the vinyl format of 45s—what, for you millennials who never played them, were the smaller records with the bigger holes in the middle. It was a smash, reaching number two on the *Billboard* charts, and opened the door to promote the B side as a single on the radio too. That was unusual. Most of the time, record companies would put out what they were going to push as the hit on the A side and not care much about the B side. In the case of the B side of this record, it was Ritchie's rock 'n' roll rendition of a song traditionally played at weddings in Veracruz. You probably know it well. I'm talking about "La Bamba."

What Ritchie did was ingenious. Not a Spanish speaker, he learned to sing the lyrics phonetically and then translated the rhythm into rock 'n' roll with his guitar. As José Feliciano would explain, "'La Bamba' is a great song because it's easy to sing, and the way Ritchie Valens did it was really cool. Ritchie's version crossed over because it was simple and Americans could sing 'la bamba' even if they didn't know the rest of the words. 'La, la bamba' was all they needed."

He raises an essential point about how this new sound of America was being shaped by Latinos and even by traditional Latin music—albeit delivered in the guise of rock 'n' roll. It didn't matter what the lyrics really meant; what mattered was how they made you *feel* listening or singing along: *"Para bailar la bamba"*—"to dance la bamba"—*"se necesita una poca de gracia."*

"Una poca de gracia para mi, para ti, ay arriba, ay arriba"—"One needs a bit of grace, a bit of grace for me, for you, now c'mon,

c'mon." You didn't know what that meant but you sang it and you felt it—that little bit of grace and you too could dance la bamba.

I can only imagine how much further Ritchie Valens might have gone and what his greater influence on music and culture would have been had his life not ended so tragically—only eight months after his recording career had begun. At seventeen years old, he was touring the Midwest with rock 'n' roll stars Buddy Holly and the Big Bopper, J. P. Richardson, when their chartered plane crashed in a cornfield in Iowa. Don McLean would immortalize that day in February 1959 in his later hit song "American Pie" as "the day the music died."

Almost thirty years later, Ritchie Valens would be further immortalized in the movie *La Bamba*, a huge box office success. The film, written and directed by Luis Valdez, elevated the careers of several Latino actors, such as Esai Morales and Elizabeth Peña, and featured the sensational music of Los Lobos, a group from East LA. The title hit from the sound track rocketed to the top of the charts, the album sold two million copies, and Los Lobos—whose own eclectic sound merges rock with elements of Mexican folk music—would soon be opening concerts around the world for the likes of Bob Dylan and U2.

In later eras, Los Lobos could proudly claim their Latino roots. In the interim, however, many of the Mexican-American groups who followed Ritchie into rock 'n' roll took notice of the benefits to the name change and used a variation of the same approach. The outrageous names of rock 'n' roll bands that would pop up in the sixties gave those artists cover while still in plain view of the public.

Given the push and pull of the times, the choice to fly under the radar made sense.

In 1965, if you were sitting around at the diner with your friends, like me and my buddies, and a song came on the jukebox called "Wooly Bully" by Sam the Sham and the Pharaohs, you wouldn't have guessed there was anything Latino about it. But you knew it was catchy and would not have been surprised when it climbed to number two on the Hot 100 behind the Beach Boys' "Help Me, Rhonda." In their publicity shots, there were no clues to the real identity of Sam the Sham, who stood in front of his group in a turban while the Pharaohs donned headwear that made them look, well, like Egyptian pharaohs. The act was pure spectacle and very little Mexico. But as time would reveal, Sam the Sham was really Domingo Samudio.

That same year Cannibal and the Headhunters transformed the song "Land of a Thousand Dances" when Frankie Garcia forgot the lyrics in midperformance and improvised with a "na na na na" hook that took off. The group had no known connection to their name. They happened to be a bunch of Mexican kids who came out of the housing projects of East Los Angeles and rode a wave of popularity.

A year later, Question Mark and the Mysterians sold more than a million copies of "96 Tears." The song received more than three million airplays. Question Mark was really Rudy Martinez, and the Mysterians were Mexican-Americans from Bay City, Michigan.

Ironically, at the same time that you had a funky name for a group of Latinos whose individual names were barely known, others who weren't actually Latino became famous to millions precisely because they sounded or seemed like they were. A testament to the growing appeal of Latin sounds and tastes, these non-Latinos were doing a reverse crossover to borrow elements of music, comedy, food, and culture before merging it with their American sensibilities.

If you turned on *The Ed Sullivan Show* on a Sunday night like everyone else in America, you might laugh at a comic named Bill Dana—not Latino—when he used a wacky Spanish accent to create a hilarious sketch about the next astronaut heading off to Mars: "My name is Jose Jimenez." Or if you were a gringo who discovered a fast-food stand called Taco Bell, you might have gotten your first taste of Mexican food—or at least what you *thought* was Mexican food. Or, in the early sixties, when you heard Herb Alpert and the Tijuana Brass playing an instrumental piece called "The Lonely Bull," the spirited horns meshing with the roar of a crowd made you feel like you were really at a bullfight.

Herb Alpert was not Latino. Raised in a Jewish family in the Boyle Heights section of East LA, he did grow up surrounded by Mexican-American music and influences that he absorbed while honing his talents on the trumpet. After playing in the USC marching band, he had an awakening as a musician that took place during a trip to Tijuana, where he heard a mariachi band at a bullfight. He took that inspiration and composed "The Lonely Bull"—which became a Top 10 hit in 1962. For the corresponding album, he hired a team of session players to fill out the Tijuana Brass—although none were remotely from Tijuana. At performances Alpert used to joke to his audience that the group was made up of "four lasagnas, two bagels, and an American cheese." That is, four Italians, two Jews, and a white-bread American.

The group became hugely successful—as did the label that Alpert started with Jerry Moss, A&M Records, the company that would serve as a recording home for his music and that of a roster of some of the most iconic names in music. To give you an idea of Alpert's impact, over the years *his music alone* would sell more than seventy million albums.

The upshot of these reverse crossovers proved that having an accent or a Latino last name or celebrating your heritage didn't have to get in the way of success. Or so it would appear based on the fact that many of those groups with made-up names kind of came and went. Maybe, a lot of Latinos might have been thinking, it was time to proclaim who they were, where they came from, and what they stood for, and to take pride in their differences.

This was, after all, the 1960s. The civil rights movement, led by Dr. Martin Luther King Jr., was taking on the status quo for equal rights. Why shouldn't Latinos, even with their disparate concerns, be a part of that movement?

And you know what they say. The leader appears when the people need him most.

In the push and pull of these years, changes in the immigration laws of the mid-1960s significantly limited the number of Mexican immigrants who could come to America legally. But because there had been no letup in the demand for cheap labor, the laws managed to dramatically boost the numbers of undocumented workers coming over the border. Without documentation, without citizenship or legal standing, workers had no protections from injury on the job, no recourse when they were being exploited.

At issue were all workers' rights, thus connecting the cause of Latinos—in particular Mexican-Americans—to other groups at the economic margins. Thanks to the leadership of Cesar Chavez, advocating for one group led to another merger with mainstream America. These bonds did not come easily.

The tipping point for action came in September of 1965, when a group of mostly Filipino grape pickers in Delano, California, walked off the fields—demanding pay that was equal to the minimum wage. A week later, the National Farm Workers Association, led by Chavez and activist Dolores Huerta, joined the strike. The timing wasn't great. The grapes from a record harvest had just been picked and the workers had very little leverage at that point. One of the large corporations affected by the strike hired thugs to break up workers voting to unionize, and then attack the voters, overturning tables and even smashing ballot boxes. But the intimidation only served to unify the two workers' groups that wound up merging and forming the United Farm Workers of America.

Chavez then sent two workers and a student activist to follow the grapes that had already been picked to the end of their destination. When they arrived at a dock in Oakland, protesters asked the unionized longshoremen not to unload the grapes. Now you had a much larger merger. The International Longshoremen's and Warehousemen's Union, who were responsible for working the docks and who had immense pull around the country, got behind the farmworkers and refused to load nonunion grapes—leaving a thousand ten-ton cases of grapes to rot on the docks.

Chavez took the next step by setting off on a three-hundred-mile walk from Delano to the state capitol in Sacramento to pressure the government and the farm owners to respond to the workers' demands. Along the way, his aim was to also wake up the general public to the workers' plight.

To that end, he called upon a successful playwright and director to tell the story of their cause. Luis Valdez—the same writer/director who would later bring *La Bamba* to the screen—was actually from Delano and had begun working as a migrant in the fields of California at the age of six. Valdez took part in the mission, founding the Teatro Campesino to spread the workers' message through performance—both to the workers themselves and to those interested in the outside world.

Though it would be years before an acceptable collective bargaining agreement would be made, Cesar Chavez, Dolores Huerta, and others, like Luis Valdez, had begun to build the architecture of a movement that would grow in strength and voice over time. The Chicano movement expanded from workers' rights to include other issues such as the importance of voting, access to public education, and economic empowerment at every level.

Cesar Chavez changed the conversation for those Latinos, young and old, who may have felt that their background worked against them. His advice was "We need to help students and parents cherish and preserve the ethnic and culture diversity that nourishes and strengthens this community—and this nation."

And, without question, in the 1960s and '70s, music was the main vehicle for enriching the community and the nation with the greatest diversity of artists ever witnessed within a generation—including two masters of the guitar, one from Puerto Rico and the other from Mexico.

CHAPTER FOUR

Listen How It Goes
(Oye Como Va)

I remember listening to that cool thing Santana was doing, mixing rock with this Latin vibe. It gave me hope. To me, there is no better thing than that because you kind of open that path a little, make it easier for the person coming down the road. And, hopefully, each artist that does that will continue to do that for the artists that are coming behind them.

—GLORIA ESTEFAN

There are many, many reasons that I consider myself to be fortunate. But let's start with the fact that beginning in the late 1960s I was a blessed, lucky person to have entered into one of the most beautiful businesses in the world—the music business. The fact that I had the opportunity to pursue my dreams and begin my journey as a musician/singer and actor, to experience that path, was a gift—and one that had to happen for me before I made the life-changing decision to channel my passion and work behind the scenes. My thought was that I could still be successful in the business of music, yet retain my same drive for success on behalf of other artists, fulfilling dreams vicariously.

So that was the path that I chose. And my further fortune was having the ability to hone my sensibilities and my ears while studying all the music breaking out at the time. I also had the chance to see how certain career decisions could alter the trajectory of artists for much better or much worse.

Take the decision by José Feliciano in 1968 to cover "Light My Fire" by the Doors. Blind from the time of his birth in Puerto Rico, Feliciano was one of eleven boys, and had come with his family to Spanish Harlem in 1950, when he was five years old. He taught himself the guitar, practicing for as many as fourteen hours a day, and, with his perfect pitch, began to sing after being inspired by vocalists who were gaining renown in rock 'n' roll. His career began modestly after he dropped out of high school to help support the family and started to play coffeehouse-type places around town. Before long he was discovered and signed to RCA. His first recordings were in Spanish and quickly made him a star in South and Central America, across the Caribbean, and in Mexico. That was when RCA brought in producer Rick Jarrard to make a record with Feliciano that could translate to the domestic market. When Jarrard heard the intriguing version of "Light My Fire" that José had been performing in concert, he thought that could be the gold they'd been looking for.

It was a huge risk to cover a rock idol like Jim Morrison, even more so to recast the song on José's acoustic guitar and with completely original vocal phrasing—less than a year after the Doors record had been a number one chart topper. But José's rendition knocked everybody over. And when I say everybody, that *includes* Jim Morrison.

José's version hit the pop charts in the summer of 1968. The timing was brilliant. The corresponding album was a mainstream success. Another wall came tumbling down for a Latino artist. José Feliciano would proudly recall, "I was the first to have two albums on the charts at the same time. One was in Spanish and one was in English. After 'Light My Fire' became a hit, all of a sudden my Latin albums resurfaced. So I had two types of music on the charts at the same time." A few months later, in the fall of 'sixty-eight, at the age of twenty-two, he was invited to sing the national anthem at the World Series.

Another decision was at hand as to how José should sing the anthem—an opportunity that came about after he was recommended by the Detroit Tigers announcer Ernie Harwell, a legend in the broadcast booth who also wrote songs in his spare time. Ernie and José never discussed how José should sing it either. Apparently Ernie didn't know what was supposed to happen when José walked out on the field for game 5 between the Tigers and the St. Louis Cardinals, led by his guide dog, Trudy, and holding his acoustic guitar, before being seated in front of an orchestra that was probably expecting to accompany José in standard fashion.

José loved the anthem but had made the decision not to deliver it in standard fashion, sensing that people in the stands really just wanted to get on with it. So he did the opposite of what Ritchie Valens had achieved with "La Bamba." Ritchie had taken a Mexican classic and strained it through his rock 'n' roll guitar. José took the ultimate American classic and let it slowly pour out through his acoustic guitar.

It didn't have the Latin flamenco jazzy feel that José had used to propel "Light My Fire." The anthem he performed had a soulful, bluesy touch. It was emotionally elegant, respectful, and beautiful. But nobody at Tiger Stadium that afternoon in a crowd of mostly white males—wearing suits, white shirts, and ties—had ever heard anything like it.

The orchestra behind José didn't quite know how to follow— and so they didn't. They stood by and watched. Nobody in the live crowd of the national television audience knew how to react to what they were hearing. But as it would turn out, the consensus was that the anthem had been somehow violated. This was, after all, at the height of the protest movement against the Vietnam War; some would say that altering a national treasure like that could be unpatriotic. The applause was lukewarm and José could sense that his performance had not gone over well.

He was right. War veterans watching at home threw shoes at their TV sets. The angry response filled the national news, provoking even more outrage. José was baffled. Looking back, he would recall, "I didn't intend to cause such controversy. But sometimes when you're an innovator, it's like being an inventor. If the invention takes hold, it could be controversial. There was talk about deporting me. Deporting a Puerto Rican—that's an interesting concept. We're American citizens! It would be like deporting a Texan. How do you deport a Texan from the United States? They couldn't deport me. But there were consequences. My records stopped being played on the radio. I had to go to Europe to make a living because in the United States bookings became scarce."

So there was a short-term backlash against an artist like none other to perform the beloved national anthem in a rendition like none other. However, in the long term, the performance set a precedent that has become so much a part of our culture we tend to think that life has always been that way. You can see it at every major sporting event when any artist, famous or not, takes the mic to sing the anthem as it has never been sung.

We now wait to hear how the artist will interpret the melody and soar to the musical peak—*"o'er the land of the free!"* We may even pause beforehand to remember the renditions that have shaken the house in the past like Whitney Houston's at the Super Bowl. Unique personal expressions of the anthem started with José's version. But at the time it was one more sign that the times were a-changin'.

Its influence would be radicalized less than a year later on a rural field in upstate New York before half a million people, many of whom had flowers in their hair, were smoking dope and rolling around naked.

Woodstock, 1969. It was a new day. Let's start with the rendition of the national anthem that Jimi Hendrix played on his Stratocaster that bent, twisted, wrenched, warped, and screamed the notes in a way that made José's version mild by comparison. It was a defiance of the status quo and a departure from following musical, cultural norms. As such, Woodstock was the perfect stage for a Latino who'd never even released an album to leave his mark on everyone who was there: Carlos Santana.

Listening to Santana would always be like looking into a kaleidoscope of places and times. Carlos was born and schooled in Jalisco, Mexico. His dad, a mariachi violinist, made sure his son practiced the violin for two hours a day as a boy, and by the age of eight Carlos was playing on the streets of Tijuana for coins.

As a teen, Carlos was exposed to the blues of Muddy Waters, John Lee Hooker, and Ray Charles, and one night at a concert he heard the electric guitar. He watched the movement of fingers on frets, linked them to sounds, and could almost play the instrument before his fingers ever touched the strings.

When his family moved to San Francisco in the mid-sixties, new sounds were thrown into his musical alchemy: psychedelic rock coming from the iconic concert hall—the Fillmore. Carlos went to performance after performance. He drank in the Grateful Dead and Jefferson Airplane as well as jazz pioneers like Miles Davis. And when Carlos didn't have the money to buy a ticket, sometimes the promoter Bill Graham would catch him crawling in through the back windows.

At picnics in the area Carlos would hear every strain of Latin music being played—Puerto Rican, Afro-Cuban, Cuban, mariachi, and jazz music—and he would dream of fusing all those diverse sounds into one. That sensibility would dramatically influence his guitar playing and give it that one and only Santana sound you identify the moment he has played only a few notes. But his path to becoming known as the one and only Santana was then still uncertain.

As the story goes, his break came one night when the lead singer from a group showed up for a concert at the Fillmore on a bad acid trip and was unable to perform. Frantic calls went out to other musicians to fill in and, making a pivotal decision, Carlos volunteered, was allowed onstage, and delivered a guitar solo that stunned the audience.

Bill Graham championed Carlos and what became his band, and later on when the promoter was desperately needed to help out with the logistics at Woodstock, he agreed to assist only if Santana and his group could play in prime time. Carlos took some LSD early on the day of his scheduled performance, figuring he'd come down by the time he was called onstage, but the group was whisked on in advance, and there is really no way of describing the eleven-minute instrumental known as "Soul Sacrifice" other than to echo Carlos' own belief that he doesn't make music—it just comes through him. When the mixture of spiritual, hard-driving, cranked-up, psychedelic jazz, blues, and his Mexican roots came together on that stage, his name instantly became synonymous with Woodstock—the launchpad to what is today a career like none other, one that has connected him to multiple generations across five decades.

Cheech Marin described that moment of his arrival in the cultural landscape by saying, "Santana came and—boom! All bets were off, man. When we hit the hippie era it was the first case of you not being put in a little section. He was obviously Mexican, and the music was obviously Latin music. But it was obviously hippie American. The people all went for it, and barriers started to come down. The people all started getting together and they got stuff from each other—especially through music. White people listened to Santana. And we listened to the Grateful Dead."

Soon after Woodstock came Carlos' first album release with its Top Ten single hit, "Evil Ways." Then, in 1970, Santana's second album, *Abraxas*, contained two monster singles, "Black Magic Woman" which peaked at number four on the *Billboard* Hot 100, and a song that broke all the rules: "Oye Como Va." First of all, it was a rock smash hit that was all in Spanish. Secondly, it was neither an original song Carlos had written in Spanish nor an update of a traditional Mexican song. In fact, "Oye Como Va" was composed by none other than Tito Puente and had been released seven years earlier as a record that was embraced by the Latin music market and that Carlos Santana chose to reinterpret and deliver up to the American mainstream, elevating his career and, at the same time, connecting Tito Puente to a much larger audience.

You might not have known how to translate the words—*"Oye como va, mi ritmo"*—"Listen how it goes, my rhythm"—*"Bueno pa' gozar, mulata"*—"It's good for having fun, mulatta"—but you felt them, you sang along, you were hooked. In one record you had a fusion of a Mexican rock guitarist's faithful rendition of an Afro-Cuban-inspired composition by a Puerto Rican master of the timbales—as Latin as Latin music could get and at the same time a hit that would be a bridge into the biggest rock music trends of the 1970s.

Those kinds of artistic decisions really can make or break careers and ultimately have the potential to change the world, as far as I'm concerned. And, wouldn't you know it, right at this very same point in time, after having trouble getting airplay, José Feliciano roared back to life thanks to a song he wrote that was partly in Spanish and partly in English.

The decision came about, José would later recall, when he agreed to make a Christmas album, again with producer Rick Jarrard. "Rick told me I should write a Christmas song, and I thought to myself: That's going to be tough. You know, you're competing with 'White Christmas' and some of the great songs of all time."

But as he started to hum melody, inspiration struck, and the idea for "Feliz Navidad" evolved. José Feliciano recognized that the time was right for a bilingual anthem of goodwill to all. He noted, "I think the fact that it was in both languages really took it over the top. People didn't feel alienated because it was only in Spanish, or it was only in English—it was like bridging a gap."

A recent *Atlantic* magazine feature on the impact of "Feliz Navidad" on popular culture over the past forty-five years also commended the experience of watching seventy-year-old José Feliciano perform it today:

> . . . in watching him, you don't see an artist who entered the mainstream while in some ways operating on the fringes as a Latino musician from a US territory. You see a man whose fingers move across the fretboard as though dancing. A man who, though he cannot see his audience (Feliciano is blind), nonetheless inspires them to stand up and dance and sing along from, yes, the bottom of their hearts. What you won't hear is a single boo.

"Feliz Navidad" brought people together through the joy and spirit we all love about the holiday season. And not only did it bridge a gap between Latinos and non-Latinos; it also allowed Latinos to connect with one another in a way that wasn't always so common. Again, in these years Latinos weren't really identifying as such or connecting to one another as part of a broader community.

Those divisions were not going to go away entirely. Don't get a Puerto Rican started about why you can't lump him or her in with Cubans. Ask a Mexican and they're not sure anybody who isn't Mexican can even be Latino. Lest we forget the expression about Latinos, they were still in many ways united by language, divided by beans.

But when it came to "Feliz Navidad" it didn't matter what kind of beans you preferred. It didn't matter if you were born in a home in Puerto Rico that didn't have indoor plumbing and came to the mainland for work opportunities that could lead to a better life. Didn't matter if you were a Mexican migrant who'd come to pick fruit. Or if you were a member of a Chicano family that had been living in Texas for hundreds of years on land formerly owned by Mexico—which meant you crossed no borders to become an American citizen. As the saying goes, the borders crossed you. Or, as we're about to see in the next chapter, it didn't matter if you were from a well-educated and wealthy family from Cuba that had been stripped of rights, land, and privileges when Fidel Castro took power in 1959. It didn't matter whether you arrived as an unac-companied Cuban minor in the Pedro Pan program in the early sixties, or whether you arrived in subsequent decades to flee political persecution.

"Feliz Navidad," like "Oye Como Va," belonged to every Latino. Both songs threw out the welcome mat to all Americans to join in the party—Listen, how it goes, my rhythm, it's good for having fun.

Who could say no?

CHAPTER FIVE

Salsa, the New American Sauce

I was in Japan one time and I was crossing the street with my band and Celia's music was coming out the door of a little club. I'm thinking: Is that salsa music coming out of that little hole-in-the-wall? In that moment I was no longer in Japan. It was like I was in my living room with my mom and dad having coffee. It was like this flag. Celia Cruz was our home.

Celia had a lot to do with who I am as a man. There are people who are born to represent more than themselves, to represent a people. She had her own struggles, you know. Coming up, a woman of color. She kicked everybody's ass. You did not want to go after her. She whupped your ass, and she did it with a smile.

—MARC ANTHONY

As my career in the music business continued to take shape in the 1970s, my affinity for Latin music still was rooted in all the exposure my neighborhood in the Bronx had given me. In my twenties, that passion was stoked even more as so many of the salsa artists took center stage—and took the celebration of a new sound to a whole new level.

To best describe how salsa landed on the musical and cultural map, I have to start in Miami, back in the day. When I first flew down to Miami with my family in the fifties, the city was 80 percent Caucasian. A single traffic light led to the airport. I doubt whether you could have even found a cup of Cuban coffee in the terminal back then.

But today everything has changed. Back then, the world's largest airline, Pan Am, had a hub in that airport. Pan Am no longer exists. Now Miami International Airport is a Latino Hong Kong. More international cargo comes through this airport than any other in the United States. It's as much a part of the US as it is the gateway to Latin and South America. Anybody who steps foot in that airport immediately understands that it's like no other in America. That's as clear as the scent of Cuban coffee coming off the stalls . . . and the Spanish and Brazilian-Portuguese accents flowing through the long corridors.

As diverse as the Latino population is in Miami, with immigrant communities from across the Caribbean and South and Central America, Cuban-Americans still account for over half of the city. Not every single Cuban landed in Miami, but on the whole, after everything changed on the island nation on January 1, 1959—when rebels led by Fidel Castro toppled the government of Fulgencio Batista—an exodus of Cubans went streaming in that direction.

Over the years, as I came to spend a great deal of time in Miami, one of the things I noticed that's distinctive about Cubans is how passionately they cling to the soil—as I would hear so emotionally while getting to know Emilio and Gloria Estefan.

Emilio could remember how in Cuba, shortly after the revolution, soldiers came to his home and herded his extended family to the back patio while they went in search of money they suspected was being hidden in the house. When they found a safe behind a painting, the soldiers blew it open with dynamite—only to find a few pieces of jewelry and some old documents. In attempting to leave Cuba, one of Emilio's aunts was imprisoned for trying to help a cousin get a visa. Meanwhile, another aunt and uncle had left the island and made it safely to Miami. So when an opening arrived for the family to leave for Spain and plans were made for Emilio and his father to go first, Emilio remembered lying in bed in silence, looking at the ceiling, trying to remember every inch of the home he'd never see again. He was six years old.

As the airplane took off for Madrid and he left his mother behind, there were no words to communicate what Emilio was feeling—only tears. From then on, music became his way of expressing himself when words failed. Later on, his father sent him alone to Miami to live with his aunt, and it would be years before the entire family could reunite.

Stories like his help explain one aspect of the distinctions between different immigrant groups. Unlike many who come to the United States seeking a better way of life and opportunities to evade poverty, many of the Cubans who arrived in this country in the sixties in the wake of the revolution would consider themselves to be exiles from a homeland that called them to one day return. Many were highly educated, well-to-do professionals who did not grow up dreaming of immigrating to the US. They were forced here after their land and position had been taken from them, and there was a commonly held belief that it was only a matter of time before the politics shifted and they could return to the island. Rather than being in a rush to assimilate, Cubans often held on to their language and culture. Older generations didn't necessarily want to learn English because, some may have felt, they wouldn't need it once they returned home. Those who came later or who were born in later generations may not have felt the same way. Yet that deep-seated longing for a return to their original soil seems to be a part of the Cuban-American cultural DNA. And nowhere can you hear that longing and connection to roots expressed more passionately than in the richness of Cuban music.

This was embodied in the legendary Cuban songstress Celia Cruz, the Queen of Salsa.

Although Cruz had begun her recording career in Cuba in the late forties, she didn't become famous until the fifties when she took over as lead singer of the Cuban orchestra Sonora Matancera. Initially, there was some doubt as to whether or not a woman could fill the shoes usually belonging to male lead singers in those days. But Celia Cruz's extraordinary instrument of a voice soon silenced the critics and she was pivotal in the orchestra's success, leading to the international tours that soon followed. They were in Mexico, in fact, at the time of the revolution and decided not to go back to Cuba during the upheaval. Instead they waited and made their way to Miami from there.

Despite her stardom and musical stature, Cruz was soon branded a traitor by Castro and not allowed to return—not even for her mother's funeral. Years later, she would get the chance to visit the US naval base on Guantánamo Bay and scoop up a handful of Cuban soil. She kept it for the rest of her life and would ultimately be buried with it.

That's what I mean by clinging to Cuban soil. You could feel it throughout Miami and whenever you heard her voice. Anyone who was lucky enough to see Celia Cruz in concert may recall that the essence of her personality comes through in a single word. She would belt it out at every performance to the roar of the crowd—and it wasn't in English.

"Azúcar!"

The tradition started after Celia ordered a cup of Cuban coffee at a restaurant in Miami and a Cuban waiter asked her if she'd like sugar. Celia told the waiter that he should know better than to ask, that you can't drink Cuban coffee without it, and she began to joke about the exchange when she performed. This was about as far as you could get from Sam the Sham and Question Mark and the Mysterians. There was never a question of where Celia Cruz or her music came from.

For the next forty years of her career after her arrival in the United States, Cruz's influence touched every aspect of music and an array of performers who grew up listening to her. Jennifer Lopez summed up her *azúcar* essence this way:

It was always about being happy; that's what her music was about. Some artists sing about love; others sing about politics. Everyone has his or her topic. But Celia's was about celebrating life. Living your life to the fullest and not letting a moment get by you. Celia Cruz is the Queen. She represented so much joy and happiness through her music about her culture.

Comedian George Lopez recalled Cruz's indomitable energy, above all, saying she was "tireless, almost like a Bruce Springsteen. I saw her a few times. One night, it was one o'clock in the morning and she was still going."

That Afro-Cuban energy that Celia Cruz embodied and the *azúcar* zest for life were some of the ingredients in the list that were being cooked up in the early seventies as salsa music was heating up the scene. Some of the other elements and cooks in the kitchen are worth identifying as well.

Tito Puente used to shake his head and roll his eyes when he heard the word "salsa"—which literally means "sauce" in Spanish. To him, the music had the same mambo rhythms he'd been hearing and playing for years.

But there were innovations and expansions that distinguished salsa and can perhaps be traced through the connection between Xavier Cugat and a young musician from the Dominican Republic named Johnny Pacheco back in the late fifties. Pacheco could play flute, clarinet, and saxophone and was classically trained at Juilliard. He was earning good money in Cugat's orchestra, but he became bored with the limited repertoire that had been carefully honed and tested into a winning formula for its audience. While Cugat was traveling on business, Pacheco spiced up the saxophone arrangements with another musician and set the orchestra off on a new sound. Cugat was not happy about this when he returned, and Pacheco was asked to leave.

As upsetting as it must have been for the young Dominican to be let go, he did the entrepreneurial thing and turned lemons into lemonade—or in this case, he took some of those musical ideas and went on to launch his own label. What a country, America.

Pacheco started Fania Records with an Italian-American lawyer from Brooklyn named Jerry Masucci who also happened to be handling Pacheco's divorce. Masucci had fallen in love with Latin music on a trip to Cuba, and as one marriage ended, another partnership began. They each put up 2,500 dollars, worked out of a broom closet in Masucci's law office, and sold the albums the company produced from the trunks of their cars.

Arriving just in time for the cultural revolution of the sixties and seventies, Fania became a musical melting pot of its own, drawing from the well of talent spurred by over a million Latinos now in New York City, much in the same way that Motown came to life in Detroit and created a crossover sound that changed music history. So how would you define Motown? By the artists, musicians, writers/producers, and arrangers who created the music. Or, as Berry Gordy, founder of Motown, would say, it was a stew made up of "rats, roaches, soul, guts, and love."

Similarly, as Fania assembled their roster, salsa was best described by who was cooking it up. We're talking about a revolving group who became known as the Fania All-stars, the Latin music dream team—Pacheco, Hector Lavoe, Ray Barretto, Willie Colón, Bobby Valentin, Rubén Blades. When Celia Cruz joined to perform with the All-stars, wow. You built on the music's Afro-Cuban and Spanish roots, added in the dimensions and feelings of players who were Puerto Rican, Dominican, Panamanian, and so on. And then, as salsa evolves, you welcome everybody else to add their own flavors and you get touches of Mexican folk music, mariachi, and more, and even tweak it with rock 'n' roll, and you have a sound that feels different and new and yet honors everything that went into making it.

Whatever you wanted to call this collaboration that was deliciously marinating, by 1973 everybody wanted some. After selling out events at smaller venues in New York City and larger arenas in Central and South America, Masucci and Pacheco decided to gamble on a concert in Yankee Stadium. It was one thing to fill a nightclub in Manhattan, but filling sixty thousand seats at Yankee Stadium was another. On top of that, they had to put up what for them was a huge deposit to ensure the security of the field, as the Yankees were about to return from a road trip. Masucci feared they were going to lose their shirts . . . and their pants.

The event didn't sell out. But somewhere between 45,000 and 60,000 showed up for the concert and they started going crazy early on when Ray Barretto and Mongo Santamaria launched into a conga battle on "Congo Bongo."

The more Pacheco pleaded with the crowd not to enter the field, the more they came down from the stands, so much so that the police couldn't contain them. The emblematic moment of the night came when a girl started dancing on top of the piano that was holding fireworks to shoot off later in the evening. Loco! Right then it was time for everyone onstage to flee before everything blew.

According to the massive word of mouth, musicians ran toward the dugouts and the clubhouses and the concert came to a halt. But the buzz kept on, building passion that spread the gospel of salsa far and wide.

In the large scheme of things, salsa represented the transition from the dominance of the kings of the nightclub—bandleaders like Xavier Cugat and those who followed in his footsteps—to what would later emerge during the Latin Explosion where we would see an individual artist like Marc Anthony selling out multiple dates at Madison Square Garden. It was the segue to pop, setting the stage for a moment in 2014 when a Latino superstar, singing only in Spanish, would sell out Yankee Stadium for two consecutive nights.

And there you go.

In the smaller scheme of things, during its heyday, sparks of salsa would soon be finding their way into other mainstream genres of seventies music—including disco. Let's not forget too that in the early disco days the clubs were mostly underground and very much a part of a counterculture that was friendly to gay, Latino, and black patrons. Even as the decade wore on, and everybody in the mainstream had to learn how to "do the Hustle," the music in the discos and on hit records still drew heavily from Afro-Latin percussion and a syncopated, sped-up beat that incorporated the irresistible pulse of salsa.

But still, no matter how salsa flavored other music forms, it managed to retain its original, authentically Latino voice.

Not to be outdone, there were regions in the country other than New York and Miami where Latino artists were giving voice in their own way, both in music and other forms of entertainment. On the West Coast, a band by the name of Los Tigres del Norte—formed by brothers who came to California after their father got injured and could no longer ranch in Mexico—pioneered a style known as norteño. The brothers used their accordions to fuse *corridos* and *rancheras* into long ballads with morals in ways that were both traditional and not. The stories they sang about dealt with the most pressing issues affecting their community—the drug trade, gangs, immigration woes, and life in *el barrio*. In a song like "Jaula de Oro" ("The Golden Cage"), they tell the story of an immigrant who lives in fear of being discovered without papers. His children have forgotten the Mexico that he cannot forget—but to which he cannot return. And so he lives in a cage with the fear of being deported, and although the cage is made of gold, the lyrics tell us, it is still a prison.

Los Tigres del Norte held up a mirror to the real struggles of the people who followed them. They were not just talking to a fringe community but rather leading a protest movement through music. Along the way, the group would sell more than *thirty million* albums over the next four decades and continue to this day in their music and in their political activism.

Moving forward, contributing to the community and to the nation, Los Tigres have preserved the past too, keeping it alive in song and in custom. Some of their concerts have lasted twelve hours, starting at night and ending in the morning. The norteño style has become part of Chicano culture that really started to cross over into the English-speaking mainstream in the same era when other kinds of storytellers made their way into the recording booth.

Cheech Marin—whose real first name, it turns out, is Richard—was apparently funny from birth. "When I was born," he used to say, "my uncle looked into the crib and said, *'Ay, parece un chicharrón.'* Chicharrón is deep-fried pigskins—all curled up. So my nickname became Cheech."

He grew up in Los Angeles, the son of a policeman and the nephew of Rudy De Leon, the highest-ranking Chicano in the LAPD at the time—who would later have a police station named after him. Cheech would say that the reason his dad became a cop was because he wasn't allowed to advance in the Department of Water and Power. According to Cheech, cable splicer was as far as you could go if you were Mexican. You might say he had his own internal push and pull going on with his father, a policeman, on the one hand, and stories in the newspaper on the other, that highlighted negative stereotypes of Mexicans.

At the same time, music was a huge influence in his Los Angeles household, where Cheech grew up listening to Ritchie Valens and Frank Sinatra and eventually becoming a singer and a guitar player. And then he met a Chinese-Canadian who had a Motown hit named Tommy Chong. The two first teamed up to go into music—which informed everything they did—at a time when marijuana and stoner culture became popular, and soon they were coming up with material that was as mainstream as the munchies at four a.m.

Cheech's point, looking back, was "You didn't have to be any race or nationality to be a stoner. You could be from Kyrgyzstan or Tibet or Venezuela or Madagascar. They have stoners everywhere—and I know because I've gone there."

In the early seventies, Cheech and Chong benefited from great timing, as not only was stoner culture in its heyday but FM radio stations began to flourish, many replacing AM radio for audiences who cared about the sound quality for listening to music. "FM" stands for "frequency modulation"—which allows for high-fidelity sound. Younger audiences, along with others, turned to FM in droves, and these stations were able to provide a whole new way of listening.

Cheech explained, "AM top forty was tightly controlled. We got though on FM. There was little or no control over it, and that's where Cheech and Chong came in. We were FM darlings. It wasn't a minute-and-thirty-second song, followed by a minute-and-thirty-seven-second song. It was long cuts and long albums. You had never heard of anything like Cheech and Chong on AM radio before. 'Basketball Jones.' 'Sister Mary Elephant.' All of a sudden—boom! People couldn't get enough of it."

Coming from a musical point of view and building their audience on radio, Cheech and Chong built their comedy through rhythm and cadence that let you into the club of being a stoner and Chicano, even if you were neither. Their humor was infectious.

How can you not laugh at something like "It's not even the drugs that'll kill you, man. What really kills you is looking for drugs"? Kids and young adults everywhere in America could recite their routines verbatim—which would eventually tally up at nine hit albums and eight hilarious movies, including *Up in Smoke*, which was the highest-grossing movie of 1978. The two cowrote and starred in all of their movies and Tommy Chong directed most of them.

And in that comedy space, they could push the envelope like the stand-ups that they were, for example, doing a bit that involved Cheech making up a song that played on the stereotype of Mexican-Americans but then turned it on its head: "Mexican-Americans don't like to just get into gang fights . . . They like flowers and music and white girls named Debbie too."

Cheech figured out how the humor translated. He explained, "The lines were so true and so funny. And everybody got it. You'd sit in a movie theater the first time people heard it and you'd hear screams of laughter. Sometimes you couldn't hear the lines because they were laughing so hard. But it identified a truth in a funny way. That truth was, we are part and parcel of the culture. We go back and forth. We're seen as the other. But we're intertwined. We get what the deal is."

In addition to an award-winning acting career for Cheech that continues to this day, he has distinguished himself as an author, a Chicano activist, and a leading art collector. As an iconic voice who has contributed to the cultural sharing that has led to the new sound of America, Cheech Marin understood the power that humor had for creating common bonds between people who are different but who can come together to laugh.

Humor can be as disarming as music. We all witnessed that very phenomenon in the mid-seventies when a sitcom called *Chico and the Man* introduced a lovable, sharp-witted comedian named Freddie Prinze to a national audience.

Freddie initially took some crap from the Chicano community for playing a kid from the barrio of East LA. That's because Freddie wasn't Mexican—he was part Puerto Rican (his mother) and part Hungarian (his father). But the chemistry between Chico and an old, curmudgeonly, bigoted American mechanic living in a garage, played by Jack Albertson, soon made it the top-rated show on national television.

It had been a quarter of a century since *I Love Lucy* and there had been no TV role for a young leading male Latino since Ricky Ricardo. Freddie Prinze was an example to kids growing up that making it to the big time—via television and comedy—was possible. That's what Freddie represented to George Lopez.

George would recall that to him, Freddie Prinze was closer than family. George's father had left home two weeks after George was born, and his mother paid him scant attention throughout his childhood. George once wrote to Warner Bros. Studios as a boy and achieved his dream of getting two tickets to watch a live taping of his hero acting in *Chico and the Man*—and his mother refused to take him. How crushing.

Then came a day in January 1977 when the world was shocked by devastating news that Freddie Prinze had shot himself, leading to his death the next day. Brokenhearted, George Lopez took it so personally that he eventually made a pilgrimage to the cemetery where Freddie was buried and found the grave site. He bent over in tears, and when he touched the plaque he noticed it was a little loose . . . and he pulled it out and took it home with him. Years later, when Freddie's widow found out, she said: "I always wondered what happened. But of all the people who could've taken it, I'm glad it was George."

It would be more than two more decades before George Lopez built his stand-up comedy act into a hit TV series—the first time that a sitcom about Latinos, played by Latinos, had been back on network television. But just as Freddie Prinze, as well as Cheech and Chong, had handed the baton to George, he would prove the viability to the general marketplace of Latino-flavored comedy—making a spate of TV series possible today.

That's what happened in the transformational 1970s when there was a new commingling of Latin influences that appealed to the masses. The group Malo released "Suavecito," which some called the Chicano national anthem. Simon and Garfunkel sang *"I'd rather be a hammer than a nail"* to the tune of the old Andean folk song known as "El Cóndor Pasa." And a couple of years later Simon brought a Latin vibe to the hit "Me and Julio Down by the School-yard." The Tejano singer Freddy Fender had a big hit with "Wasted Days and Wasted Nights." And by the end of the decade, Julio Iglesias had moved from Spain to Miami to bridge the gap between his platinum career and the English-speaking market. Soon he would team up with Willie Nelson to release a duet called "To All the Girls I've Loved Before" that went to number one on the country charts and was an unmistakable sign that the two cultures were merging.

That was the new American sauce and it just tasted good to everyone.

CHAPTER SIX

Miami Sound Machine

The greatest thing human beings have is the ability to communicate and to express different points of view.

—EMILIO ESTEFAN

If you take a pin and stick it somewhere in the year 1976, I'd have to say that was when I began to sense the early tremors of a Latin music infiltration in the general marketplace—one that could actually lead to something bigger, an eruption of some kind. It wasn't even on a conscious level but certainly from the standpoint of a guy straddling a job in the music publishing business and my new role as a manager working with artists who were more in the pop and R&B categories. I couldn't ignore the influence of Latin rhythms and instrumentation being incorporated in almost every musical genre.

Most telling was the music of a group I came across by the name of Dr. Buzzard's Original Savannah Band. Made up of a dozen kids from the streets of the Bronx, they had a bold, bright sound that reflected the musical influences of the neighborhoods where they came from and honored roots that were Latino, black, white, and mixes of all the above. As musicians they ran the gamut from big band jazz to Latin disco, presenting not only a distinctive sound and artful songwriting but some of the most theatrical visuals of the time.

Looking at them, what you saw was less of a band than the appearance of a carnival, as I used to describe them. Their costumes were not actually costumes; that was their street clothes, what they wore. How refreshing in an era when fashion was driven by the disco look. The band's front man had the whole zoot suit look down, morning, day, and night, while some of the other guys in the band wore baggy pants with old newsboy caps. The lead singer, Cory Daye, wore vintage dresses from the forties and fifties. But more than all of that, Cory had a voice and a vocal style and a way of phrasing that was so distinctive, making her one of the best stylists I've ever worked with.

When I first saw the band, they had been turned down by a handful of labels, which was unbelievable to me. Passionate about their potential, I went to RCA and made the pitch and we got going. The Savannah Band then wrote a song called "Cherchez La Femme," which started with the line *"Tommy Mottola lives on the road . . ."* My first shout-out. Crazy, right?

Besides the wild reality that it made me a famous name from the moment the record hit the airwaves, the record took off immediately and practically defined the musical moment. Something about the music, the production, the time period, and Cory Daye's singing all came together to create one of those hit songs that let everybody remember where they were when they first heard them.

In New York City, I remember being amazed at hearing it coming out of every bodega in the Bronx, every upscale West Side boutique, every car radio and nightclub. The big problem for the group was that overnight fame can be a recipe for failure if you're not ready for the challenges that come with newfound fame and money. Just the exposure that I got from having my name in the song was a heady experience that could have derailed my career if I hadn't sought to stay grounded. But that was not what happened with the kids in this band, unfortunately. The Savannah Band was like a tank of gasoline and success was a match. They started fighting with one another, climbing out windows on hotel terraces, and having all kinds of complications that ultimately led to a meltdown.

For me, however, there were important lessons across the board in how to develop, manage, record, and promote talent. Plus, I had just witnessed how music with multicultural influences could attain such widespread popular appeal. I'm not saying that a lightbulb went off in that same period at the end of the seventies that sent me looking for that kind of multicultural sound that could cause a change in the entertainment industry. But not too many years later, when I first heard Gloria Estefan and the Miami Sound Machine, I had this powerful reaction that led me to think they were everything the Savannah Band might have been.

I thought: There it is . . .

Not long after that period in 1976 when I first started to work with the Savannah Band, a serendipitous meeting took place at a wedding in Miami.

In those days, Emilio Estefan had already made his way from Spain and had started a group called the Miami Latin Boys that happened to be performing at said wedding. Earlier, when he first arrived and started working in the mail room at the Bacardi company at the age of fifteen, he didn't understand English, not even "Go to the third floor." Working hard to learn the language, he also sought work in music—playing the accordion at the time, and eventually putting together this particular band that played at clubs and communions, bar mitzvahs, *quinceañeras*, and office parties. And the Miami Latin Boys got so good they were asked to give pointers to young talent around town.

So at this wedding in question, a young woman approaches Emilio to tell him that he'd once given her some tips that had been very helpful. Emilio, pleased, invites her to the stage to sing, but she says no.

"Go on, Glorita," says her mother, standing nearby. "You sing beautifully."

Glorita was Gloria Fajardo. She had no plans to be a musician. She had just finished a degree in psychology at the University of Miami and was working at Miami International Airport as an interpreter. After arriving in the United States at age two, Gloria had gone on to become perfectly bilingual, moving between Spanish and English as effortlessly as walking from one room to the next. Besides having studied French in college, she had been accepted to study international law at the Sorbonne in Paris—and was on her way to becoming a diplomat.

Somehow, Gloria was convinced to get up onstage to sing with Emilio and the Miami Latin Boys at that wedding. And, as you probably can guess, she never did get to the Sorbonne. It's easy now, after the tremendous success that Gloria and Emilio have had, to see the hand of fate in their meeting. But there were many obstacles that needed to be worked through as the band that she joined shortly after that evolved into the Miami Sound Machine.

After starting to gain some traction, Emilio and Gloria got a deal with a smaller label that put out a record with the A side in Spanish and the B side in English—that was their mix. Let's not forget that by the time the two met, Miami was officially bilingual. Cubans constituted more than a third of the city's population and every governmental form in Miami had to be offered in both English *and* Spanish. As the Miami Sound Machine, of course they would want to capture that duality, right?

But when they moved up the ladder and were signed by CBS/ Latin, they were told to throw out the English and make a big push in Spanish.

That was *not* their vision. But it was very difficult for them to control their own destiny back then. By the early eighties, the music industry was starting to consolidate and smaller indie labels were going by the wayside as corporate consolidation meant larger record companies that needed to control artistic output and their investments. However, to do that, the label needed to push Emilio and Gloria forward. Problem was, much of the time, it didn't.

Emilio remembered, "Sometimes I used to fly to New York to meet with CBS. I once spent the whole morning and afternoon waiting in the lobby. I didn't have money to stay in a hotel. By the end of the day, the people there would never even see me. I don't even think they cared, which was even worse."

Gloria would later say that they had to fight at every turn because everyone told them that they had to pick a lane and stick to it, that being known for music in two languages would never work. Nobody knew how to market them either, saying that they were "too Latin for the Americans" and "too American for the Latins." But they kept on pushing. Gloria explained, "The easiest word for anybody to give you is 'no' because they don't want to take any risks. They want things fed to them in a very easy way. So when we tried to tell people, 'Okay, this is us. This mix of the percussion, with the horns and the dance music, this pop sound,' they would say, 'No, you have to take out the horns, take out the percussion.' At one point, during the time of the boy bands, somebody told Emilio, 'Take out the lead singer girl.' They even said that 'Estefan' is too difficult to pronounce and asked us to change our name. But we kept saying, 'Listen, this is who we are!'"

What fueled their convictions, she would say, was that "we had our own sort of focus groups. During our gig days, everybody who could possibly be at a party was listening to us—many different nationalities—and we could see from their reactions that we really appealed to them all. So we knew for a fact that the music would work. It just took convincing the people who were at the label and in control of the radio."

Just to complicate the challenges they were facing in getting support from their record label, there were other crosscurrents in the early and mid-eighties that bear mentioning. First there had been the Mariel Boatlift of 1980, which had created a kind of backlash against Cuban-Americans and other Latinos, especially in Miami. This was the response by Fidel Castro after ten thousand Cubans demanding permission to leave the country had locked themselves in the Peruvian embassy in Havana. Fidel had mockingly granted this request and basically told anybody else in Cuba who didn't want to stay to get the hell out. As a flotilla of 120,000 refugees streamed toward Key West, President Jimmy Carter and the Cuban community opened their arms.

It took a while before people realized that Castro had used the opportunity to empty his jails and rid his country of criminals and the mentally insane. The deluge of immigrants overwhelmed social services in Miami, the crime rate began to soar, and furious white and black voters responded by passing an English-only ordinance, ending the city's official bilingual status. In that inflamed environment, Caucasians in Miami then went in front of television cameras to say they wished for all the Spanish speakers to leave. The rhetoric heated up on national talk shows with an implied question being asked: Whose country is this, anyway?

During this turbulent time, Miami Sound Machine continued to raise their profile, recording albums and touring extensively to support those releases. In the process they attained enormous success—outside of the country. By 1984 they were huge international stars, ambassadors of music that was authentically American and authentically Latino, and still pop. But without the support and understanding from their label, they had yet to attain their big breakout hit domestically.

When they came up with a hot dance song in English called "Dr. Beat," the label didn't believe it would be a hit. So Emilio spread it out through DJs and weeks later it was huge as far away as Holland. Naturally, the Miami Sound Machine went to tour in Holland—and, through a series of in-the-moment decisions, struck a new kind of gold.

In those days, Gloria recalled, "Emilio would whip out his accordion and he would play a medley of legit Cuban congas that went back hundreds of years. It didn't matter who you were, if you were in a tuxedo or a dress, jackets and shoes got flung off and it was a free-for-all on the dance floor. We were playing at a club in Utrecht, Holland. The place was packed. We played 'Dr. Beat' and all our English songs, but the crowd wanted more and more. But we had no more."

Emilio suggested to her, "Let's play those Cuban congas." Gloria reminded him, "But they don't speak Spanish." To which he replied, "So what? They don't speak English either. They speak Dutch. What's the difference?"

So they played the congas and a free-for-all ensued, just as it did at all of their gigs. Afterward, Gloria had a brainstorm: "We're standing outside at three in the morning, and I say to our drummer,

'You know, this rhythm is part of our lives. We need to write a song that celebrates it, and talks about it in English.'"

The drummer, Enrique Garcia, wrote it on the tray table on the plane to their next stop in London. As soon as they got back to Miami and did an arrangement, they started playing it and everywhere people flocked to the dance floor in droves.

Gloria described what happened next, saying, "We talk our Latin record company into letting us do an album in English and they give us twenty-five grand—which was ridiculous. So we put in another forty-five that we had in savings. And that's how 'Conga' came out. But even after this song won at the Tokyo Music Festival, the record company still didn't want to release 'Conga' as the single! They chose a different song from *Primitive Love*. We told them, 'You're making a mistake.'"

They then went ahead and released "Conga" as a single in Europe. "It took a year to circle around and reach the top of the charts in the States," Gloria remembered, "because, again, the recording company didn't believe in us. So this song, which Alvin and the Chipmunks are now doing, and which gets played at probably every wedding known to mankind, had to come through the back door."

That distinct blend of Afro-Cuban rhythm with great orchestrations, some pop, and a beat that could sweep everyone to the dance floor was deceptively complex. When Gloria was invited to perform on *The Tonight Show*, Johnny's band had to be tutored by the horn players of the Miami Sound Machine to get the syncopation.

It was almost as if America had been waiting for something like this—a single definitive song that blended a Latin rhythm and English lyrics so fluidly that it could burst through the doors of any wedding reception as an invited guest. An anthem song, it took you over the moment you heard it.

Rita Moreno tells a funny story about the first time she heard "Conga." She was in her car, listening to the radio, and she started bopping from one direction to another. She looked up and saw a policeman comically waving a finger at her as if to say, "Careful, lady. . . ."

But the best story of all was the reaction to "Conga" that took place in Burlington, Iowa, when Gloria and Miami Sound Machine sang it to more than eleven thousand people who broke the Guinness World Record by forming a conga line on the banks of the Mississippi River.

And the people who broke that record were not Latinos. These were Iowans in the heart of corn country. What else is there to say?

Throughout the eras, my trajectory and that of Latin music seemed to have been running on separate tracks. Latin music had always been in my sights though never my focus. But in 1988 that changed when there was a collision that happened after I was brought in to head up Sony—what had been CBS Records before being bought by the Japanese. At thirty-nine I was the youngest guy to ever be made president of a record company of that size and I had everything to prove. Meeting Emilio Estefan—who became a brother to me—provided the collision that was integral to everything I would build at Sony, starting with the opportunity to take Gloria under my wing, and beyond. From that collision on, I became deeply immersed and connected to Latino music and culture.

My closest encounter with the reality that this music was shaping the new sound of America was witnessing the reaction to *Mi Tierra* from all different audiences. Without a doubt, it spoke to Latinos and Spanish-speaking audiences the world over. But music lovers who didn't speak a word of Spanish loved this album too. It was as if it had helped cause a shift in cultural curiosity. Why wouldn't someone in the mainstream be as hungry to savor this music as they might be to taste Cuban black beans and rice?

That was my thought a short time after we put out *Mi Tierra* when Emilio came to me with a tape of the music of Israel "Cachao" López, a living legend. Already in his seventies, the legendary Cuban bandleader, bassist, and composer—known as the true inventor of the mambo—had been living for years in exile in Miami. Emilio told me that Andy Garcia, the Cuban-born movie star and musician, was producing an album with Cachao and many music legends.

Emilio made the case for why we should distribute the album. "Look," he said, "this is great. Listen and you'll see." He went on to add that Cachao was revered as the god, the maestro, by everyone who followed in his footsteps. I listened to the tape and agreed. The fact is, I loved Emilio and trusted that he would only ask for an artist of the stature that Cachao truly was. Not only did I sign Cachao, but I believed in the project one hundred percent. The album, *Cachao: Master Sessions Volume I,* was a knockout, won a Grammy award, and for Latin music aficionados is a classic. A sequel album, *Volume II,* followed.

In this same time frame, guitarist Ry Cooder recorded *Buena Vista Social Club* in Cuba, reuniting many other names in Cuban music who had never left. Proving the power of music to endure, the album was also widely embraced by an increasingly diverse audience.

American mainstream tastes were definitely changing. So much credit goes to Gloria and Emilio Estefan. "Conga" did it.

CHAPTER SEVEN

Selena Interrupted

I grew up in Corpus Christi, so we were "Selena Town." It was a common experience to see her on a Saturday night in a small dance hall. I remember going to her concerts, watching her, and dancing. She was the epitome of what it meant to be a star. Seeing that growing up made you go, "Wow!" I loved all of her songs. I loved her Spanish-language music before she did the mainstream stuff. Like myself, she didn't grow up speaking Spanish. But she sang in Spanish, and felt really tied to her culture, yet she was totally American too. She learned Spanish later on, and so did I. Her experience is my experience. Growing up with Selena was like growing up with my identity.

—EVA LONGORIA

Latino visibility across different fields really began to pick up steam in the 1990s. In addition to Latinos in music, food, sports, and comedy, new Latino names were coming into renown as filmmakers, actors, and TV show hosts, as well as fashion designers and business entrepreneurs. I would argue that the more opportunity that arose for Latinos to distinguish themselves as celebrities in popular culture, the more they were embraced by greater numbers of non-Latino Americans—and the more opportunity was being created for all Latinos to excel.

Some of the progress took place in fits and starts. After Ronald

Reagan's enactment of the 1986 Immigration Reform and Control Act (IRCA)—policy intended to crack down on the pipeline of undocumented workers flowing over the border to fill the demand for labor in agriculture—the (perhaps) unintended consequence was that three million immigrants, mainly from Mexico, were given amnesty. It was a great day for so many Mexican-Americans who had worked in the shadows for years, even as long as decades. But in a boomerang effect, eight years later, California passed Prop 187, a punitive law that banned undocumented workers from receiving most health care, education, and other public service benefits, making it a felony to in any way manufacture or assist in the sale of identification papers, and requiring state and local law enforcement to report possible illegal immigrants. Two years after that, Latino activists would succeed through legal action to have Prop 187 declared unconstitutional on the grounds that immigration is only under the authority of the federal government.

Amid that push and pull, new voices had come forward to call for greater participation by Latinos in the electoral process. The activism of Willie Velasquez in San Antonio in the mid-1970s had led to voter drives and lawsuits to achieve greater voting rights. In the same time period, Congress had passed the Equal Educational Opportunities Act, which made it possible for Latino students to access bilingual education in public schools. And so, as the combined result of educational and political empowerment, at the dawn of the 1990s, Latino leaders began to gain prominence at the highest levels of government. There was Antonia C. Novello, the first woman and first

Latina to become surgeon general, appointed by President George Herbert Walker Bush. Then, under President Bill Clinton, two Latinos—Federico Peña and Henry Cisneros—were named as secretaries of his cabinet (Peña as secretary of transportation and Cisneros as secretary of housing and urban development). Throughout Clinton's two terms, twenty-five Latinos, an unprecedented number, would be appointed to positions requiring Senate confirmation.

So with all this change, how did you get the word out about these huge stories of progress and challenge? Well, I would argue that it was through the Latino celebrities of music, popular culture, and, increasingly, media that honored Spanish-speaking and bilingual audiences. For years, the Latino grapevine had existed in Spanish-language newspapers and in music-dominated radio shows at the commercial and college campus levels. Once the nineties got going, television stations that were either owned or run by Latinos were gaining significant traction.

Take the growing importance of a show hosted by Cristina Saralegui on the network Univision. *El Show de Cristina* became *the* place for talking about Latino issues and showcasing Latino talent, young and old. A Cuban-born immigrant, Cristina was instantly adored by audiences for her charisma, energy, and honesty. Her show allowed artists to tell their stories over the course of an hour, giving them a space to tell viewers who they really were—which provided a powerful connection to audiences when combined with a performance on that platform. Cristina soon became a star at what she did. In fact, when she visited Oprah Winfrey's show at

Winfrey's studio in Chicago, Oprah had Cristina stand up in the crowd and paid her great respect. "This lady says she's the Oprah with salsa. Not true. I'm the black Cristina."

The development of Univision had come around the same time I took over at Sony Music, and both the network and Cristina's show would be tremendously helpful to our artists in the coming years, although at first it was probably difficult for anyone to understand how powerful Univision would become.

The name does suggest how they approached their multifaceted viewership. Univision took news and events going on in twenty-three different nations, covered the stories individually, then tossed them together like a salad and put them on one platter for all to see. This allowed Latinos from different countries to understand their unique relationship to one another. Notably, this was a time in the United States when children started to come of age in homes of mixed backgrounds. If someone with a Mexican father and a Colombian mother was talking to another kid with a Puerto Rican father and a Dominican mother, it became all the more expedient to identify themselves as Latinos. Cristina understood those dynamics and also understood the threat that Latinos posed to the powers that be and how different demographics of her audience might see those from other countries of origin as rivals.

Cristina recalled:

> Everybody was coming here, and there was a lot of competition for jobs, so there was a lot of hate. On top of that, the people in power did not want Latinos to be united. They didn't want them

to have any power as a voting bloc. Nobody in power wanted a big bloc of a huge minority controlling anything. So they would divide and conquer. That was what I saw when I started working—division and hate. Univision did a lot to soften that. And to teach the people from one country about the other, and about all the good things that we brought together. We are from many different places, and everybody came to love the music from everyplace else. A winner is a winner. Doesn't matter whether you're from Venezuela or Cuba. We became each other's role models. Television gets a lot of credit for making that happen.

Cristina should also get a lot of credit for raising issues of importance to Latinas, challenging the status quo in the Latino community on issues like domestic violence and sexual assault, while empowering women in general. As a champion of all Latinas in entertainment, Cristina's show served up a feast of their many different offerings—including the music of a young female Tejano singer who in the early 1990s was on her way to major stardom.

Tejano music, also known as Tex-Mex, is as crossbred a type of music as any. It grew up in Texas way back in the 1800s when Eastern European settlers were moving in alongside Mexicans, creating a sound that would later include everything from polka to mariachi and Mexican *cumbia*, and other Latin influences of the *conjunto* and *ranchera* styles. By the 1980s and '90s, Tejano had also become infused with country and western, blues, rock, R&B,

and pop. You can hear the influences of Tejano, which was defined less by those influences than by who was playing the music, on everybody from Freddy Fender to Los Lobos and Ry Cooder, to the young singer known forever by only her first name. Selena.

Selena had built a solid following in the eighties while touring Texas and Mexico with her family in a band called Selena y Los Dinos. The road to success wasn't necessarily an easy one, and it was fortunate that her father, Abraham Quintanilla, had overcome obstacles that gave him a vision for his daughter.

As a young man, Abraham had begun singing Mexican doo-wop, apparently at a time when Mexicans weren't interested in hearing doo-wop. So as his kids began to show musical gifts of their own, he decided to go back to more traditional musical roots. After leaving a job at Dow Chemical to open a Mexican restaurant in Lake Jackson, Texas, he designated a space next to the dance floor as a stage where his three kids could perform. His son, and oldest, A.B., was the guitarist and creator of the music. The middle child, Suzette, became the drummer. And Selena, identified with perfect pitch by age three, was out front singing at the age of nine.

The restaurant was forced to close when business dried up during the recession of 1982, and the family was on the verge of applying for food stamps. But Abraham managed to remodel a bus to take the band on tour. Never before had there been a young female Tejano singer at traditional beer-sponsored events throughout Texas and Mexico, and for a time organizers at some of these events refused to even book her.

Selena learned her craft through performance after performance, and she homeschooled herself along the way to get a high school diploma. The band played in just about every tiny hall around Texas, and finally, in 1989 after amassing a strong fan base in her hometown of Corpus Christi, Selena got her first recording contract, with EMI. It's interesting to note that early on, Selena didn't speak Spanish and had to learn to sing phonetically, just as Ritchie Valens did. As her popularity grew, however, and she started being interviewed for Spanish-speaking media, she stepped up to embrace the language and become fluent—so as to be able to converse across cultural divides.

That first album, *Selena*, sold briskly, setting up a second album, *Ven Conmigo*—the first by a Latina Tejano singer to go gold. With "Como La Flor" as the signature song of her next album, *Entre a Mi Mundo*, Selena was on her way to the career breakthrough that came with her fourth album, *Live!*, which won her a Grammy for best Mexican-American album. And then in 1994, Selena began to extend past the borders of Tejano with her *cumbia* hit "Bidi Bidi Bom Bom." This song, about the palpitations of a woman's heart when she saw a certain guy, pushed her fans toward Latin pop. And the album that it was on, *Amor Prohibido*, would supplant *Mi Tierra* on the charts and, ultimately, become the top-selling Latin album in the US of all time.

After the smash of "Bidi Bidi Bom Bom," EMI decided that her success in the Latin market had proven she was ready for a crossover. Wasting no time, Selena began work on the album *Dreaming of You*.

During an appearance on Cristina's show on Univision in this time period, twenty-two-year-old Selena talked about her plans for the future. Her dream, she told Cristina, had never been to be a singer—that was her daily reality. Her dream was to have her own business and be a fashion designer, and Selena had turned that into a reality too, going as far as sewing the rhinestones on the bustier that became her trademark onstage. Selena had already merged her passion for design and business by opening two boutiques in Corpus Christi.

Cristina commended the work ethic behind Selena's success and the independence Selena had shown in her decisions—whether in choices having to do with music or in her personal life. In fact, the first time she wore her beaded bustier, her father was shocked and demanded she change. Selena stood her ground and created a fashion trend. Then came the big rebellion when she fell in love with a member of her band, Chris Perez, against the wishes of her father. When Selena and Chris eloped, Abraham was beside himself. But Selena smoothed over her father's feelings and convinced him to welcome his son-in-law into the family. On her show, Cristina brought out the traits she saw as so admirable in Selena:

> CRISTINA: Do you believe you are very strong?
>
> SELENA: I believe so, dominant and aggressive.
>
> CRISTINA: Dominant and aggressive?
>
> SELENA: You have to be.
>
> CRISTINA: Why?
>
> SELENA: There are a lot of men in this business. If you can't speak for yourself they are going to run you down every which way.

CRISTINA: You think if you weren't a strong person in this business the people would take advantage of you because you
are a woman?

SELENA: Exactly. It has happened! I also have the protection of
my father.

At the time of that interview, Selena's plan was to start a family
once she had completed her much-anticipated crossover album, due
to be delivered in July of 1995, and the European tour that was
being scheduled to promote it. All the stops were being pulled out
as she began recording the songs—in English, by Grammy-winning
writers—and in early 'ninety-five she performed to a sold-out
Astrodome.

As I had seen before, many young artists get knocked off balance by fame and adulation early on. But the security in Selena's
family life, combined with her raw talent, pointed toward a future
without limits—especially when you realize that a whole segment
of the American population wasn't really aware of her at the time
and was on the verge of joining her legion of Latino fans.

If anyone looked like they were about to have it all, it was
Selena.

Tragically, as we know now, that day never came. Instead, on
an awful day in late March 1995, Selena was shot and killed by the
president of her fan club after the woman had been caught embez-
zling funds. At only twenty-three, Selena had every possibility in
front of her. The world was hers to go after and there's no telling

how far she would have gone, where her path would have taken her and the impact that growth might have had on others.

But I would also add that even in her short time here, before her life and career were tragically interrupted, Selena had attained a legacy that would never die: a lasting change in the perception of the kind of music she sang (as evidenced by the five million copies of her English-language album that was released posthumously) and a new respect for the potential of female artists in a male-dominated genre like Tejano/Tex-Mex. Or any other.

Not only that, but out of the massive expression of love that followed her death, a new recognition was born about the growing strength of the Latino market. As a matter of fact, when *People* magazine published a story after Selena's death, they opted to have it translated into Spanish alongside the English account. That was a breakthrough. The editors ran a follow-up story on the cover of their West Coast issue while the East Coast covers carried a story about the television show *Friends*. They were shocked to find that not only did Selena outsell one of the most popular shows on television, but that her picture on the cover completely sold out.

The editors then decided to put together a special commemorative edition on Selena's life, which went through two printings and sold more than a million copies. This time, Selena outsold editions that had been printed after the passing of Jacqueline Onassis and Princess Di. All of this, in turn, ignited plans to create an entire magazine for *People* in Spanish. *People en Español* is now flush with more than six million readers, and is a leading brand in the Latino market.

Two and a half years after she was killed, Selena's life was immortalized in a film that dramatically elevated awareness of her contributions to the new sound of America. And it didn't hurt the movie's success that a controversial choice was made to cast a young Puerto Rican dancer turned actress from the Bronx in the title role.

The account of how Jennifer Lopez's career took off after doing justice to Selena's life story on-screen is another essential part of the buildup to the Latin Explosion. Before I recall those details, there's one more part I have to tell first that really led to the lighting of the fuse.

CHAPTER EIGHT

La Vida Loca

Before that night, it was a subculture, a genre. The culture already had a life of its own, but when Ricky Martin took the stage at the Grammy Awards, it changed the game.

When Americans saw it, they said: "We don't know what that is, but we want some of that! Whatever he's doing we want to be part of that thing right there." It opened the doors wide open and people were asking themselves: How do I become a part of that thing?

—ARTURO NUNEZ,
DIRECTOR OF APPLE'S DIGITAL MARKETING FOR LATIN AMERICA

There are certain moments in time that clearly separate all that came before and all that is about to come afterward. The evening of February 24, 1999, was one of them.

Culturally, that year's Grammy Awards ceremony was a seminal moment for all Latinos, whether they knew it at the time or not. Hosted by Rosie O'Donnell, the show boasted the star-studded presence of legends like Madonna and Sting, and also featured a performance by an artist from Puerto Rico named Ricky Martin—who was nominated in the category of Latin pop. For me, the way it all played out, making history that most readers may well remember, the night was also the greatest validation of everything that I had believed was possible from the moment that Gloria Estefan had convinced me to give the go-ahead to *Mi Tierra*.

None of it had happened without a crazy amount of heavy lifting. Ricky's journey alone was an epic endeavor, starting from his days of growing up in Puerto Rico. In talking about his ancestry, Ricky would acknowledge that his roots went back to Spain and Corsica—what was half-Italian and half-French. "It's incredible," he'd point out, "because it's likely that some of my grandmother's ancestors hopped on a boat and went to New York. And today they are considered Americans—while others left Europe and ended up in Puerto Rico. Because of that, I'm considered Latin." Then Ricky would ask the question, "So when did I stop being Anglo and start being Latin? Or vice versa? Who knows?"

What we do know is that Ricky grew up in San Juan understanding that a spoon and a can of soda were a great excuse to make music. The spoon also made a great microphone for a six-year-old, and that's how Ricky started—singing along with 1970s records by bands like Led Zeppelin that his older siblings played. He started out as a kid actor in Puerto Rico, doing commercials and such, before the chance of a lifetime came when he auditioned for Menudo.

The word "menudo" actually refers to a Mexican dish made of cow stomach, or tripe. The boy band Menudo, however, was a Latin pop music phenomenon that was started in 1977 with six Puerto Rican boys who would eventually generate the same hysteria as "Bieber Fever" to masses of Spanish-speaking adolescent girls. Menudo was able to last for over three decades because of a rotating roster of talent. Once the kids turned sixteen, they were replaced by younger performers. Genius. They were forever young and constantly reenergized with new faces connected to changing pop music trends. At twelve, Ricky's first two auditions were disappointments. His singing and dancing were fantastic but he was considered to be too small. But he got a third shot and worked his magic. Overnight he was plunged into the reality of what it took to be a star performer. Apparently, after being told of his acceptance into the band at seven p.m. one night, by the next morning he was on a plane to Orlando to begin learning eighteen dance routines, all while conducting media interviews and conferring with stylists.

There probably couldn't have been a better training ground for Ricky to break through the barrier between cultures and set off the Latin Explosion. Besides the five years of conditioning that made him have to work at a highly disciplined level during fourteen-hour workdays, the travel exposed him to different cultures around the world. Although Menudo was a Latin pop band, it recorded in other languages—including English, Italian, Portuguese, and even, for the Philippines, in Tagalog.

Ricky's attitude was that language wasn't an issue. He insisted, "If it's about breaking boundaries and uniting cultures, I'll do my best. If I need to sing in Mandarin, I'll try."

After graduating from Menudo in 1989, he continued with a broad-based show business career—acting in soap operas in both Mexico and the United States, on Broadway in *Les Misérables*, and eventually starting a solo recording career. Guess where. Yup, at Sony, on our Latin label, where he had steadily been ascending, especially after the release of his hit song "Maria," which surged through Latin America and set up his European following. By the late nineties, we started talking to him about doing an album in English and crossing over. Why not? To me, he embodied the incredible energy of all of the icons of Latin music, combined with an Elvis Presley sex appeal that could not be denied.

As always, timing was critical and so was finding the right song and the right platform to introduce him to a whole new audience. A pivotal opportunity came up when he was asked by FIFA, the governing body of World Cup soccer, to compose a song for the 1998 championship tournament hosted by France.

A fan of football, as it is known everywhere but in America, Ricky didn't need to be told how big this opportunity was and how intense the anticipation was for the World Cup, which only took place every four years. The song Ricky came up with was "La Copa de la Vida" and it not only met that excitement but then wildly exceeded it. Soon enough, the album it was on, *Vuelve*, would go through the roof, selling an eventual twelve million copies— everywhere but in the US. The international reaction was a phenomenon. Ricky remembered, "I could feel something very powerful happening. It was about the possibility of uniting cultures through music, music that made people feel so comfortable with it that it didn't matter where you were from."

Clearly, this was the groundswell for his crossover. But for some reason, as incredible as the song was, just before his performance of it at the World Cup, FIFA told him that, due to internal politics, he might not be permitted to sing. When Ricky happened to announce this to the press, upsetting FIFA execs, the organization responded by not letting him know if he could perform until just before the final game. When FIFA did tell him he could go on, they attached crazy conditions: no stage, no dancers, no lights, no special effects. In short: no production whatsoever.

With little time to spare, Ricky reacted the way Desi Arnaz might have. He put together an orchestra, dressed them in black and white to help them stand out against the green field, then grabbed the mic before the championship game and organically transformed a worldwide audience at the Stade de France into the backyard of a gigantic house party.

Aerial shots of Ricky's performance looked like twenty ants dancing around a piece of cake left on a picnic table. But it didn't matter. The music was so soaring, his energy so contagious, that Ricky and "La Copa de la Vida" filled the entire stadium with a celebration that had nothing to do with the game. The pure joy in Ricky's performance had the Three Tenors—Luciano Pavarotti, José Carreras, and Plácido Domingo—cheering him on from the stands and dancing along.

We were blown away. If he could create such a reaction without any props or visuals, I could only imagine the potential of a performance on a large-scale platform that had the right production values. The perfect opportunity to do that arose when the album was nominated for a Grammy.

We then went immediately to the committee that runs the Grammys, making the reasonable request for Ricky Martin to perform live onstage during that show on national television to introduce him to the mainstream American audience and the world—singing his global hit, which was in both Spanish and English.

The Grammys weren't interested. Even after millions had reveled in Ricky's World Cup performance in France, the committee members didn't get Ricky's appeal to the American public. They told us he wasn't the right fit. They actually thought people would flip to another channel. I cannot tell you how exasperated their words made me feel.

Therein lies the reality that Latinos had been dealing with for decades. In fact, only a few months later in 1999, Latino groups would call for a brownout—a boycott of CBS, NBC, ABC, and FOX to protest the lack of brown faces on network television. This was before anyone saw George Lopez on his sitcom. It's crazy to think how so much talent was being denied.

Here Sony had one of the most dazzling artists in the world, so striking and handsome, with great style and fashion, singing an incredible hit song with amazing rhythm. It was a pop masterpiece that made people stand, sing, jump, and scream. And these execs at the Grammys have no interest? What didn't they get? When you hear music that is so sensational it deserves to be performed live on a Grammy stage, how can you not get it? Especially when the album it's on has been nominated for an award.

So we go back to the Grammy committee. I say, "Are you telling me that if we have the same world-class artist who's lifted people across the globe to their feet, and we take that same hit song in Spanish and have him sing it in Spanish *and* English, that it's not going to blow the roof off the show and be the biggest hit in America?"

Their comeback was to remind me of all the other superstars whose labels were fighting just as hard to get them onto prime time. They couldn't see risking one of those slots on a lesser-known artist in a category that didn't have the same interest as others.

There it was—their fear and belief of keeping everybody in their box. And there was my response to that—bullshit! So we did what you do when the competition got bloody for a slot on the Grammys by leveraging all of our Sony muscle to make sure Ricky Martin got to perform on that stage. That year alone, our artists would include Lauryn Hill, the Dixie Chicks, and Céline Dion—who would win two awards for her song from *Titanic*.

Thanks to that strategy, obviously a risk on my part, which combined with much commotion and arm bending, and the help of the show's producer Ken Ehrlich and CBS president Les Moonves, Ricky Martin did step onto that Grammy stage that night. All my predictions and promises to Les that this kid would deliver never looked so good.

The horns lifted the roof of Radio City Music Hall from the start. A Latina pounded out the beat on a drum over dancers emerging from under fabric through a poetry of motion that grabbed everybody's eyes. Then a giant staircase was pushed onstage along with a square life-sized box that was spun around to reveal Ricky in black leather pants, a gray shirt, and a smile that won over the crowd before he sang a word. It was love at first sight. Women, men, young, old, straight, and gay. Didn't matter. Ricky had that thing, that thing, that thing . . . raw, pure sex appeal. Not unlike Elvis wagging his hips on TV for the first time.

The sound of Ricky singing "La Copa de la Vida" swept everyone away. *"Do you really want it? Do you really want it? Here we go! Olé! Olé! Olé!"*

He'd performed this song hundreds of times before. But at Radio City Music Hall, filled with the biggest names in music in the world, this was a first. And the crowd jumped to their feet in appreciation, almost immediately. The brass band and backup singers were on fire, and accompanying musicians came down the aisles rattling tambourines and banging on drums like it was a carnival as women onstage in costume and circus stilts added to the party by twirling streamers. Over and over Ricky pointed to the crowd and asked the question: *"Do you really want it? Do you really want it?"*

By the time he climbed to the top of the staircase and threw open his arms to end one of the best Grammy performances ever, the answer was clear. Yes, America was in.

The shock waves were still reverberating through the hall when Rosie O'Donnell walked onstage and asked: "Who was that cutie patootie?" Heading backstage after the show, I was right next to Madonna, who turned to me and said, "I have to meet him immediately!" That night, moments after they met, she and Ricky agreed to record a duet.

Overjoyed as I was that very next morning of February 25, 1999, it was impossible for me to put what had happened the previous evening in perspective because my mind was focused on two basic questions. 1) How could Ricky get the most out of the opportunity he'd just created? and 2) How many other Latino artists could Sony get through the opening to reach this new audience that was going to want more, more, more?

The magnitude of what had really just happened couldn't be measured until later. Comedian George Lopez would put it into context, saying, "When Michael Jackson moonwalked for the first time, it really changed not only Michael Jackson; it also changed music. When Ricky Martin came out on that Grammy stage, it changed Ricky Martin's life, clearly, but it was also a huge moment for Latinos."

Cristina Saralegui, speaking as the Latina Oprah, had this to say: "That was the night when Americans went, Oh my God! Ricky was very cute, and very charming. He was shaking his bon-bon; he really knows how to do that. And everyone was saying, Look at this Latino kid! For the first time Americans realized what Latin talent was. For the first time! I guess people just didn't understand the kind of talent we had. I had been around Gloria and Emilio long enough to know what worked. So I knew what was going to happen from there."

Randy Falco, president and CEO of Univision, would go even further, describing that performance as one of the key moments that changed the conversation about Latinos in America. Randy reminded me that "it resulted in the *Time* magazine cover, and it was the start of folks recognizing the Latin impact and influence. People started to see that there was a real change coming."

Through most of the twentieth century, *Time* was *the* most popular and trusted mirror of mainstream American culture. No doctor's office was without it. Its content shaped the national point of view, and its Man of the Year was much anticipated and a venerable honor.

For decade after decade, the magazine's readers were accustomed to seeing Latino culture through stories like the Cuban Missile Crisis, the Mariel Boatlift or through banana republics and political revolutions that meant only chaos when they reached US shores. In the run-up to Ricky's performance, that meant articles about civil wars in Nicaragua, El Salvador, and Guatemala that had sent nearly a million asylum seekers headed to the US.

The cover photo of Ricky next to the headline "Latin Music Goes Pop!" was an entirely new way of looking at Latino culture. No chaos. No political problems. No poverty. No trouble at all. It was an *appreciation* for the joys of what Latino culture was bringing to the US. And more than that, what Latino culture was bringing to the world—because the magazine's international editions were interpreting the explosion in every region of the globe. The *Time* cover line that appeared next to Ricky's photo on airport newsstands in the Far East read: "Asia Goes Loco Over Latin Pop."

With a new millennium only months away, the positive ripples in that cover story resonated far beyond Ricky Martin. Of all the pushes and pulls in the relationship between Latino and mainstream American culture in my lifetime, this was a defining pull.

Don't get me wrong. I'm not saying that it changed the opinions of people who wanted to lock down the borders and kick every undocumented worker out. But for the first time, a different message pulsed through the mainstream: Hey, this is cool!

That vibe was so much bigger than one song. Even so, I was obsessed with finding what that next hit was going to be. No easy feat, after the world witnessed how high the bar had been set. For Ricky to take things forward and exceed where we had been, it had to be *beyond* huge. And I'll never forget sitting in my office, almost stunned, when I heard the centerpiece for Ricky's next album. All I could think was: "Ohhhhhh, shit . . . here we go . . ."

It was a song with Latin flair, but also mixed in some ska—a Jamaican style of music that was a precursor to reggae—some rock guitar, horns, and percussion. It was written by Desmond Child, who'd also worked with Ricky on "La Copa de la Vida," and who now is a member of the Songwriters Hall of Fame. And it was accompanied by a video that showcased Ricky with a gorgeous Croatian model. The title mixed two languages, English and Spanish, but the song was for all the world.

The song was called "Livin' la Vida Loca."

And it shot Ricky from the Grammy stage into the stratosphere.

"Livin' la Vida Loca" debuted at number one in twenty countries. Every ticket for the attached twenty-five-city concert tour around the United States sold out within eight minutes. And they would've gone sooner, but that was as fast as the electronic system could process them at the time. The tour was then expanded in the US and around the world. Four million fans would go to see Ricky live. Twenty-two million albums were ultimately sold. The cover didn't even need a title. All it needed was Ricky's name and his image. In a matter of months, Ricky Martin had gone from "Who was that cutie patootie?" to being recognizable by just about anybody with a pulse.

The discipline that he'd gotten in those early years from Menudo helped push him through a brutal tour schedule from New York to LA, Edmonton to Atlanta, and Munich, Germany, to Osaka, Japan. This time, his travels weren't about being exposed to other cultures; they were about exposing everybody to his.

Just like Gloria Estefan, whose music allowed her to be a diplomat abroad and at home—the calling she had once wanted to pursue in government service—Ricky understood his role in continuing to change perception. He'd explain, "Some people would ask me, 'Where are you from?' And I'd say, 'Puerto Rico.' And they'd say, 'Oh, Costa Rica!' And I'm like, 'No, actually, Puerto Rico, and let me tell you about my island. This is who we are.' So, the music allowed me to educate. I don't even know if I still have a copy of that *Time* magazine with me on the cover. But at the time, that cover felt like a big responsibility. After a while, I just told myself, 'Relax, my friend. Keep it simple. Enjoy the flow and just talk about who you are and where you're from. That's all you've got to do . . .' And it was beautiful."

It was that. It made you feel that you too could live the crazy life and love it.

Ricky says "Livin' la Vida Loca" will never die, and it's pretty hard to argue with him because the song still brings great joy wherever it's played to this day.

The *Time* cover came to be associated with Ricky, Jennifer, Marc, and Shakira. But over time the Latin Explosion wasn't only about their careers and the music that buoyed them but about the explosion and celebration of Latinos across every field. Cuisine, fashion, television, film, business, sports, politics, medicine, science, technology, and more.

Along with the party associated with the explosion would be the next wave of population growth that would turn the minority that Latinos are today into the most dominant cultural force in less than fifty years.

"Livin' la Vida Loca" was the opening verse for the new sound of a new America.

CHAPTER NINE

The Latin Explosion

There was this Latin Explosion thing between me and Ricky Martin, and Enrique Iglesias and Marc Anthony. And all of us were kind of making English albums. All of us grew up in the States, speaking English and Spanish—but mostly English. So it was kind of a funny thing that they called it the Latin Explosion. As if all these Latinos came over from a far land. It wasn't like that. I was here from the day I was born.

—JENNIFER LOPEZ

A monumental opening in the music industry doesn't come around often. You didn't have to be the head of a global music corporation to know this: If you want to take full advantage of that opening you'd better be prepared to drive the needle to the edge of the speedometer. This was about to be *livin' la vida loca* on steroids.

Ricky Martin had just bashed down a door that meant our company had to work double and triple time to get out new Latino artists with new rhythms and new sounds to a public that suddenly was indeed insatiable for more.

When I was a kid I'd seen how Elvis' career was launched with a succession of hits. His songs came through the radio one after another. The public didn't have time to get tired of an Elvis song because it was soon replaced by another hit that you loved and made you want to go back and listen to the ones that came before. We'd used that same approach in launching Mariah's career in 1990. Before her first album had fully crested, we released a single from her next album so quickly that it seemed to be connected to her first.

The strategy boiled down to this: Hit the public so fast with what it loves that it doesn't even know it's getting hit. You need great music to pull it off. And we had it with Ricky Martin and "Livin' la Vida Loca." But not only that. When Ricky stamped Latin music on everyone's mind, he put us in the position to launch several artists into the stratosphere with him.

Now, in case this all sounds like an easy recipe for success, I should just back up for a moment to give you a better sense of what the stakes and the challenges really were. Let me start by addressing some of the changes that had been taking place in the 1990s, particularly in my business, with respect to trends and technology affecting not only Latino artists but everybody in the industry. First of all, vinyl (despite its resurgence years later) had at that point all but gone the way of the dinosaur; CDs, mostly albums, were dominating in units sold. Production costs were skyrocketing, which meant labels had trouble recouping their investment on lesser-known artists, unless, that is, they were promoted in the most visible way possible, right out of the gate.

But a much bigger concern was the avalanche in the works that began innocently enough with geeky technology in 1999 when a computer coder introduced a peer-to-peer file sharing service called Napster to the Internet. Any tech-savvy college kid could soon be using file sharing for free to get the latest digitally transferred music. It was the beginning of downloading and the start of the slow death of the record stores, and the end of the way the music industry had distributed its products for as long as I had been alive. For all the advances that technology does offer, this advent would be an unmitigated disaster. Things would never be the same even after Napster was subsequently shut down by federal government rulings. Within a few years, Apple would jump into the void with the iPod and iTunes, with a formula for revenue sharing with artists and their labels. Since that development, the iTunes store has become the dominant distributor of music—and increasingly, as my kids remind me every time they download a song for ninety-nine cents, not because they're interested in the artist but because they like the song, the dynamic has made it all the more difficult for a newcomer to penetrate the marketplace and fulfill his or her potential.

On the flip side, I believe that there will always be a demand for music that is authentic and flows from a place of true creativity and that adds relevance to our lives. And along those lines, we can't leave the 1990s without acknowledging the infiltration of hip-hop music and culture into the mainstream. In fact, at the same Grammy Awards show where Ricky Martin made history, we were also celebrating another huge moment when the Album of the Year award went to the *The Miseducation of Lauryn Hill*—the first time that a hip-hop artist took home that award, among a total of five Grammys that Lauryn won that night. Certainly, the Caribbean influences can even be heard in that album, making the argument that there had always been a connection and perhaps symbiosis between the growth of both hip-hop and Latin music. What's more, if you go back to that time period in the late seventies/early eighties when hip-hop music and culture were being born in house parties in the Bronx, you'll find that many of the original emcees were from Latino backgrounds.

Common, the rapper and actor, acknowledged this cultural mix in his "Like They Used to Say" by rhyming, *"Appreciate the art that came through Puerto Ricans and blacks / Speakin' the facts / the sound is much deeper than wax . . ."*

All of this is to recall the richness of the multicultural, melting-pot sensibilities of the times. And to that point, in 1999 the album *Supernatural* by Carlos Santana—featuring an array of established and newer artists that created a sound tapestry of Latin and alt-rock, blues, hip-hop, jazz, salsa, and African rhythms—blew the roof off. Aside from being a commercial and critical triumph, three decades after Woodstock the album connected Carlos to a whole new generation of multicultural fans.

Looking back, it's possible to see how the same influences that showed up on *Supernatural* would merge with the digital technology coming out of Silicon Valley and give birth to a music consumer that now has listening habits that more or less mirror the fusion in Carlos' music. Today, the largest group of online music consumers is a demographic that includes Latinos, African-Americans, and Asian-Americans. The president of Alma Advertising Agency in Miami, Luis Miguel Messianu, calls this group *fusionistas*. They simply aren't defined by any particular genre of music.

That multicultural, multiethnic audience was also part of what made the TV series *In Living Color* such a pop culture success in the early nineties. Instead of casting mostly white performers and adding a splash of color, the show's creator, Keenen Ivory Wayans, turned that standard on its head and built the cast with performers of color, adding a splash or two of white—like a guy named Jim Carrey. Always pushing the comedy envelope to the edge, the show also featured musical numbers with some of the hottest hip-hop dancing ever seen on prime time. We're talking, of course, about the Fly Girls. As a dancer and choreographer on *In Living Color*, Latina Rosie Perez earned a handful of Emmy Awards for her work on the show, as well as finding it the launchpad to a feature-film acting career.

Then there was another famous Fly Girl, a Latina from my home turf of the Bronx, who got her big break on the show in its third season. Her story is definitely the stuff that American dreams are made of.

Jennifer Lopez grew up with the inspiration of what was possible by watching Rita Moreno dance on the rooftop in *West Side Story*. Early on, she didn't see herself so much as a singer. As the middle of three girls growing up in their household—with a sister who had a better voice—Jennifer saw herself more as the athlete and the dancer.

When her parents pointed her toward college and business school, she independently chose instead to try to make it in dance, living in a New York studio apartment for a time, working odd jobs, and then booking roles in touring productions of Broadway musicals, as well as a stint as a backup dancer. The fact that she was Latina in an industry that wasn't hiring many Latinos didn't deter her. She saw her background as a way to flip the odds in her favor. Reminding herself that there weren't twenty-five thousand girls just like her out there, Jennifer decided to be herself—since there weren't that many like her. And so she made who she was her strength.

The opportunity to audition for *In Living Color* came about after getting a tip from a fellow dancer. Apparently, they had a blond girl and an Asian girl and they were looking for a Latina. She famously waited in line with an estimated two thousand other dancers vying for the one spot. Needless to say, she landed the role and became a Fly Girl for the duration of the show's run. It may be worth pointing out that rather than trying to blend in, she claimed and owned her differences, which made her a standout.

Acting seemed to be calling to her. She booked a few roles that required more serious acting chops on TV and, in 1995, appeared in director Gregory Nava's film *Mi Familia*, the beautiful story of a Mexican family that overcomes daunting obstacles to come and settle in America.

The movie came out right around the time of Selena's murder by the president of her fan club. The intense media barrage surrounding Selena's death had put her family in a painful position—with unauthorized books being written and various films and documentaries of Selena's life being shopped around Hollywood. Selena's father, Abraham, wanted his daughter to be remembered the way he remembered her, and not through somebody else's vision, and the family decided to take control over Selena's image by sanctioning a movie. They reached out to producer Moctesuma Esparza, who introduced Abraham to Gregory Nava—whose *Mi Familia* was in release and who was looking for his next project.

Even after Jennifer's work for Nava, she still had to go through a grueling audition process for the role of Selena. In fact, as soon as the casting call went out, more than twenty thousand young women got in line in five cities around the country to vie for the part. But as soon as Nava and Abraham saw Jennifer nail the audition, they were convinced that the role was hers. And for anyone who was still upset by the decision to cast a Puerto Rican to play a Chicana, Jennifer's performance put that to rest. She channeled Selena, in my view and those of critics and fans alike. As the story goes, after she reenacted a concert scene in front of a roaring crowd of real fans who seemed to be trying to keep the memory of Selena alive, Jennifer returned to her dressing room trembling and told Nava that she wanted to go into music.

Her manager and others around her did not think that was a good idea—and that's probably a kind way of putting it. Some thought it was crazy. After all, Jennifer's breakthrough performance in *Selena* had set her up for her next big break as the first Latina to earn a million dollars for starring opposite George Clooney in *Out of Sight*. That too got her rave reviews. The thinking around her was: Why jeopardize a sure thing? If her debut album were to go down the tubes, it could derail her acting career.

That wasn't my thinking. I can remember watching Jennifer in *Selena*, several times, and being wowed by her acting *and* her potential for a pop music career. And as soon as she sent a demo, I knew at once that I was right—she was a triple threat. She could act, dance, and sing. The acting and dancing were proven—and Sony had an amazing group of songwriters, and producers like Rodney Jerkins and Cory Rooney who could get the most out of her voice.

We made plans to meet at Sony's offices. Jennifer looked a little nervous when she came in, and I asked her what she wanted from her music career. She told me she wanted an A-list deal. I was happy to give it to her.

And so, three weeks after "Livin' la Vida Loca" hit the airwaves, we released Jennifer's debut single: "If You Had My Love." It was the definition of an *instant* runaway success, a number one hit not only in the US—but as far off as Finland and Australia.

The single that followed—"Waiting for Tonight"—remains her signature song to this day. Add to that the duet that she performed with Marc Anthony in Spanish called "No Me Ames." The album these singles pointed everyone toward—*On the 6*—contained hip-hop and Latin and all the musical influences Jennifer had grown up with. What moved Jennifer moved the world. The album sold millions and catapulted her to superstardom.

The stars were aligned. And when they weren't, we at Sony made sure to align them. Ricky and Jennifer appeared on *Oprah* to talk about the Latin Explosion. That reached out to a whole different audience than the *Time* magazine crowd. As Jennifer's popularity soared, her videos ran almost continually on MTV and solidified her following with that audience.

All of this was happening, mind you, in the loco syncopated rhythm of orchestrating campaigns for not just Ricky Martin and

Jennifer Lopez but also, going for a Puerto Rican trifecta, the artist whose voice transcends language—or the Latino Frank Sinatra, as George Lopez would call him.

That would be Marc Anthony.

Often, when I look back at my decision not to be a performer but to work in the business end of the industry, I'm grateful that there came a moment when I knew that no matter how good I was, that would not be enough to match up with artists who were off the charts as singers. When it comes to sheer vocal power, style, and presence, Marc Anthony is the epitome of the guy who has *it*.

Growing up in Spanish Harlem as a skinny kid with glasses, he'd spend hours in his room alone, playing the guitar and singing—because that was the only time he didn't have a problem with his stutter. His talent was so evident that his career started taking off when he was young. Latin music wasn't his thing even though his parents had played it in the house all the time. Still, in trying to get his recording career going, he thought of Latin music as too old-fashioned and even shunned it for a time.

Then a single event one night outside Madison Square Garden changed his mind. Driving in a car with the sister of Little Louie Vega—whom he played music with—he watched her put a cassette into the tape player. Marc remembered, "And she goes, 'Listen to this song. I just heard it. I think it's beautiful.' It was a song called 'Hasta Que Te Conocí' by Juan Gabriel." It was as if he had been struck by lightning. As he put it, "I heard that song and saw God.

I just saw light. It was the most bizarre, out-of-body experience. And I was like, 'Wait a minute. Can you play that again?' She put it on again and we were stuck in traffic right outside of Madison Square Garden and I couldn't help myself. I jumped out of the car and ran to a pay phone. Remember pay phones? When you had to walk around with change? I called my manager and I said, 'There's this song that I have to sing. I was born to sing this song!'"

When he told his manager the name of the song, the response was, "Well, it's in Spanish." The manager was surprised that Marc wanted to do it because he was only doing English at the time. Besides, Juan Gabriel had already recorded it. But then his manager said, "The only way to record it would be . . . I guess, salsa."

Marc went with it. "Then salsa it is," he told his manager. "I just need that song in my life."

Two weeks later, they were in the recording studio. Marc summed up what happened next:

> I had no idea what I was doing. Me and Sergio George were just sitting there looking at each other, 'cause his thing was R&B and my kind of thing was Luther Vandross. Since we both didn't know what the hell we were doing, this new sound came out that sounded like kids in New York singing salsa their way, only it came out as salsa my way. I can't sit here and take credit for knowing what the hell I was doing. We had no idea. All of a sudden, I noticed that it was cool for kids my age to drive around and play my music in their cars. It was theirs. I was them. It wasn't until I decided to record in Spanish that I realized how

much it meant to me, and that nobody could take it away from me. That it was mine. That I wasn't just an American; I was an American who had his own identity. I belonged not only to America, but to a people. I belonged to something very unique and special, something that I wouldn't change for anything.

By 1999, Marc Anthony was already ensconced with Latino audiences from his Spanish-language albums. For his breakthrough album on which he could move seamlessly between Spanish and English, we got the best of both worlds. It contained two smash hits in English: "I Need to Know" and "You Sang to Me." Then we took "I Need to Know" and rereleased it as a reverse crossover in Spanish entitled "Dímelo," which went to number one on the Latin charts.

We were imprinting in the ears and eyes of people all over the world the power of Latin music and, even more importantly, the power of Latino culture. And the numbers were flying through the roof in every direction.

This wasn't just from Sony artists, I should add. Other labels rode the wave too. Two big names that rose to superstardom in this time were Enrique Iglesias and Christina Aguilera. Enrique, born in Madrid, moved to Miami at age eight to live with his father, Julio Iglesias, after the kidnapping of his grandfather. With Julio on the road much of the time, Enrique began writing music on his own. Not wanting to benefit from connections or any of the perks of his family name, he borrowed money from the family nanny to make demos under assumed names like Martinez—which he sent out to record companies. A company in Mexico reached out to sign him, and he was started.

Christina Aguilera, the little girl with the big voice, got started on *Star Search*, moved on to *The Mickey Mouse Club* with Britney Spears and Justin Timberlake, and by eleven years old became the youngest person ever to sing the national anthem at a sporting event when she performed it at a Pittsburgh Penguins Stanley Cup game.

Cut to: 1999. In between Jennifer Lopez's release in June and Marc Anthony's in November, RCA dropped Christina's debut album with songs like "Genie in a Bottle" and "What a Girl Wants." A month after that, Interscope released "Bailamos" by Enrique Iglesias. It got a huge boost after the actor Will Smith saw Enrique at a concert and wanted to use the song in the sound track for his film *Wild Wild West*, a release on the Sony Soundtrax label. Will apparently came away from that concert thinking that the song should have been called "Gritamos" because of the sustained screaming of every woman in attendance. "It was almost like people were coming to hear him specifically to scream," Will told MTV. "Like the girls were taking turns going 'Yeah!' When one girl's getting ready to stop, she points to her girlfriend to take over. . . . Damn, just hours of sustained screaming."

This was real. Everyone wanted in. We had three amazing stars leading the way. But the one thing you learn very early in the music business is never to sit around and pat yourself on the back during periods of great success—because you're only as good as your last hit. So while Ricky was touring from Berlin to Kyoto, and while Jennifer was preparing for a starring role in *The Wedding Planner* and we were thinking about her second album, and while we were setting up an HBO concert for Marc at Madison Square Garden, I was urging our Colombian recording star Shakira to take the leap and do an album in English.

Like I said, it was *la vida loca*.

Leave it to Gloria and Emilio to bring unplanned magic to my life. Not that I needed any more magic, because the business had been all-consuming even without the run-up to the Latin Explosion. There I was, back in '98, running a multinational company with fifteen thousand employees and plenty of corporate responsibilities, strategizing Céline Dion's next move after her theme song from *Titanic* generated almost 700 million dollars' worth of sales, and juggling all of our other concerns. The last thing I was thinking about, after my marriage to Mariah Carey had fallen apart, was meeting someone new and beginning anything serious.

As I told Emilio when he tried to convince me to meet Thalia, a Mexican telenovela star and singer, "I'm not in the right place." And besides, I added, "A singer? I'm not going there again."

Thalia had pretty much the same reaction when my name came up. "Celebrity marriage? Divorced? Kids? Not interested."

But Emilio and Gloria kept working on both of us. Then, not long after Ricky Martin made his statement at the World Cup, Thalia and I arranged to get together for a drink while she was filming a movie in New York. I was sitting in one of my favorite restaurants, wearing a black cashmere sweater, and she came down the steps in a white cashmere coat and just filled the room up with light.

I wish I had a video of our first conversation. Thalia couldn't speak much English at the time and my Spanish wasn't fluent in the least. We were a comedy sketch, communicating in gestures and facial expressions. Thalia had memorized certain lines in English for the movie she was acting in and she tried to comically insert them in the conversation when she thought they'd fit. We didn't have a clear understanding about the actual words we were speaking. But if there is any proof that the two cultures could overcome a language divide and come together, it was that conversation and every one that followed.

She had to return to Mexico to film a telenovela. That took us into the long-distance-phone-call stage. Sometimes we'd fall asleep at the end of our eighteen-hour days talking to each other. This was in the period before cell phones with cameras. So we took photos of ourselves and mailed them to each other. Anyone who tells me that the cultures can't come together because of a language difference is full of it. The distance and the language barrier only made us long to be closer.

We were both so focused on our respective arenas that it actually created a balance that might have taken longer to establish. But we were in each other's corner completely. We were both amazed at how much had changed so quickly in the entertainment world as our cultures were coming together.

For example, in January of 2000, two Latino artists who were not signed by Sony—Christina Aguilera and Enrique Iglesias—performed during the halftime of the Super Bowl. A few weeks later, on Valentine's Day, Marc Anthony lit up Madison Square Garden with his HBO special. A week after that, Jennifer Lopez showed up on the red carpet for the Grammy Awards, wearing an exotic green silk chiffon Versace dress that plunged down past her navel. The dress instantly turned her into a fashion icon and changed a beauty aesthetic in this country practically overnight. Cristina made the point on *El Show de Cristina*, and elsewhere:

> If you ever see Jennifer Lopez's dresses on the award shows you realize what she brought to the culture. There would not be a Kim Kardashian without a Jennifer Lopez going first. I remember when Jenny started singing, and everyone said: "Look at that behind. Look at how fat that woman is." Look now. People are actually having behinds implanted to look like Jennifer Lopez! I happen to be Cuban, so I have a big one too. When that became fashionable, I realized even the body shape that was ideal had changed in America. When Jenny went on that stage, it became a huge fashion statement.

It was all fuel for the Latin Explosion. Yes, Jennifer sort of laughed at that phrase. But it was the red-carpet celebration to a party that had been long in coming. To keep it going, I knew it was time for the next step.

We went to the Grammy committee, to the show's producers, and back to Les Moonves, the president of CBS, and asked them all to host the first *Latin* Grammys.

Just a year earlier we had to move mountains and heaven and earth to get Ricky Martin on that Grammy show. Here we were proposing a show to CBS for a largely Anglo audience to be filled with Latino performers speaking and singing in Spanish and English. Some people thought we were nuts. But I knew if we loaded that show up with all this great talent and all these great songs, with all the color and Latin flair, that it would work. And Les Moonves bought in.

We had been moving so fast it felt like we were trying to break the sound barrier. And then, on one night—September 13, 2000—the world around me slowed down. I had the chance to sit back, reflect, and see the full impact of what had transpired in a way that was crystal clear: the first Latin Grammys.

It was held at the Staples Center in Los Angeles and aired live. It was loud; it was beautiful. It was enchanting, groundbreaking, revolutionary, and it surged through all ethnic barriers. Anyone who saw the show that night understood that culturally we were in new territory.

I'll never forget the tribute Ricky Martin, Gloria Estefan, and Celia Cruz paid to Tito Puente . . . As I watched Carlos Santana singing with Maná, Alejandro Fernández, Christina Aguilera, Jennifer, Shakira, and John Leguizamo, my mind turned back to my three-year-old self on the streets of the Bronx and the journey that we'd all been through.

My attachment to everything that had transpired was made even more powerful and meaningful when I turned and looked at the woman sitting next to me. She was Latina, born and raised in Mexico City. My fiancée. Thalia.

A few months later we were married and I became attached to the Latin Explosion in ways that will play out through my children in the near and long-term future—as it will for us all.

CHAPTER TEN

Hips Don't Lie

Latinos respect their elders more than the mainstream culture. Our elders are more valuable to us than they are to the mainstream. We understand how hard it is to get where people like Rita Moreno got, and we admire that. We listen carefully when they're asked: What did you do right? What did you do wrong? What can we do better?

—NELY GALÁN,
MEDIA EXECUTIVE AND LATINA ACTIVIST

It's true that progress never really happens overnight. Forces had been at work for decades in chipping away at many of the walls that were finally coming down. And here in the early 2000s, a whole row of them seemed to come down at once when Jennifer Lopez did something that had never been done before.

Jennifer's second album, *J.Lo*, shot straight to number one the same week as her movie *The Wedding Planner* became the top-grossing film. That made Jennifer the only musician/actor to ever have a number one album and number one film at the same time. And equally exciting, the romantic comedy that she starred in with Matthew McConaughey was a major departure from so many of the stereotypes that boxed in Rita Moreno and other Latina actresses. In fact, the original actors asked to play the major roles in *The Wedding Planner* were Jennifer Love Hewitt and Brendan Fraser. This was an all-American role that could have been played by anyone.

That liberation for Jennifer made her speak out to confront the typecasting that goes on in Hollywood. She observed, "You know, I was being offered a script and they were like, 'Well, maybe we should make her Puerto Rican if Jennifer's going to play her.' And I'd say, 'Why do we have to make her anything?' When Julia Roberts is in a movie, she is whatever she is. She's from the South or she's Irish. They don't say it as if she's white. So how about I'm just a girl? How about I'm just a person? How about I'm just a girl who works in the pet shop and is going to fall in love with Matthew McConaughey, or whoever? It doesn't matter. You know. When I started doing that, and realizing I could do that, then people started forgetting about the fact that I was 'Jennifer Lopez.' I was just Jennifer Lopez the actress. And that was really a blessing."

The crossover had been long in coming. We can't forget that Rita Moreno had to wait seven years before taking another movie role, even after winning the Oscar. The beloved Mexican actress Lupe Ontiveros played a maid in film and television shows more than a hundred times. The first Latino Academy Award–winning actor, José Ferrer, ended up disillusioned and finishing his career playing small roles on television. Ricardo Montalban, who became well-known for the popular television series *Fantasy Island* and a Chrysler commercial where he talked up the soft Corinthian leather, was so disturbed by the way he was asked to portray Mexicans that he helped create the Nosotros Foundation to advocate for Latinos in the industry. Though he received a lot of support, Montalban claimed that his role in the foundation caused him to lose work. Apparently, some in the industry felt this made him a militant.

Meanwhile, over the years the movie industry's bottom line—box office earnings—had not proven to be a sure bet for film studios to take with Latino talent or subject matter. Every now and then they took a risk. In the 1980s, along with *La Bamba* came such memorable films as *The Milagro Beanfield War*, directed by Robert Redford and produced by Moctesuma Esparza, one of the students who had helped organize the walkout of East LA high schools back in 1968. The plot of *The Milagro Beanfield War* centered around a small, agrarian New Mexican town that fights back after losing its water to powerful outsiders in a backroom political deal. It starred salsa pioneer Rubén Blades and Brazilian bombshell Sonia Braga, but didn't draw the same kind of attention as a biopic with music like *La Bamba*.

The eighties also brought *Stand and Deliver*, a movie based on the true story of a high school math teacher, Jaime Escalante, who tries to lift his students by pushing them to excel in an AP calculus class against the cynical attitude of the faculty. When the teacher, played by Edward James Olmos, empowers the students to pass the test, there is a question as to whether they cheated. The film was socially important, and the critical acclaim also led to Olmos being nominated for an Academy Award.

This same era brought other groundbreaking independent films like *El Norte*, a heart-wrenching story about two Guatemalan teenagers who head up north toward America after their father is killed and beheaded and their mother disappears. Written and directed by Gregory Nava and nominated for an Oscar in the category of best screenplay, it's a brutally honest portrayal and an emotionally riveting work. But profitwise the film didn't change the tough dynamic for getting similar movies made.

In the early nineties, a trio of noteworthy films dealt with the reality of Chicano gangs that were becoming a way of life in many Mexican-American communities, especially in the West and Southwest. With *Mi Vida Loca*, director Allison Anders cast actress Salma Hayek in a movie about gang life for Chicanas in LA's Echo Park. With *American Me*, Edward James Olmos starred and directed in a fictionalized drama that traced the evolution of what many recognized to be La Eme, the Mexican mafia, over the course of the 1950s to 1980s. A film released a year after *American Me* tackled somewhat similar turf. *Blood In Blood Out*—directed by Taylor Hackford, who had produced *La Bamba*, and written by Jimmy Santiago Baca, the Chicano poet who had taught himself to read and write in prison—told a story of three young men who grow up in East LA, one who becomes a leader in the prison gang, another who goes into law enforcement, and a third who finds his way out as a painter and muralist.

Complicating the box office calculus, they were being released in the period after the LA riots and studios worried they could inflame gang tensions. As a result, they were distributed and shown unevenly, without the publicity and support needed to prove that there was an audience for them. In truth, all three movies attained cult film status all over the world. But Hollywood basically decided that if it didn't have music like *La Bamba* or *Selena*, or comedy like the Cheech and Chong movies, general audiences did not want to dwell on the problems confronting Latinos—whether it was gang life, drugs, poverty, or prejudice. So studio execs remained skittish about getting behind a serious Latin theme and investing in Latino talent.

But something really interesting happened not long after the release of *The Wedding Planner*. Along came a gigantic movie success that happened to have lots of Latino talent in it. Not what you'd think. It was *Spy Kids* and it was science fiction comedy and family adventure. All rolled into one movie that grossed 150 million dollars.

The cast could have been Caucasian mainstream Americans as they normally would be for a film like this. But this time the kids and their parents had the last name Cortez. And the director was Robert Rodriguez.

Rodriguez had grown up in a five-bedroom stone house in San Antonio, as the third of ten kids, the son of a cookware salesman. The story that Rodriguez tells about his father gives a clue as to how he approached turning over the Hollywood applecart. If any of the kids in the family needed braces, Rodriguez's father would calculate in his head how many more sets of cookware he needed to go sell. And then he'd go out and he'd sell them. Says Robert Rodriguez: "That entrepreneurial spirit really showed us early on that if you used your imagination you could always make what you needed."

When he was eight years old, his dad gave him a Polaroid

camera, which he used to create movie stills that he'd conceived in his mind. When he was twelve, his dad brought home a video player/recorder. It didn't have a viewfinder, so he had to connect it by cable to a TV and watch the television screen to see what he was filming. But it wasn't long before he moved the television to the back door, where he filmed his brothers and sisters acting out amateur kung fu movies in the backyard.

While at film school at the University of Texas in Austin, he wrote *El Mariachi*, a film with an amusing premise: a harmless musician gets mistaken for a brutal hit man who's notorious for carrying his weapons in a guitar case. Rodriguez put it together with the same adaptability that went into his backyard kung fu films, revolving the scenes around a school bus and a ranch, and raising part of the seven thousand dollars needed to finance the project by volunteering for drug trials.

When he arrived in Hollywood in the mid-nineties, with a plan to make that movie into the bigger-budget version, *Desperado*, he found himself in a very different and difficult place.

"It was bleak," Rodriguez admitted, bemoaning the lack of Latino actors that a studio would green-light a movie for. And because no studio wanted to be the first to try casting a Latino for a Latino role and have the movie fail, they would cast non-Latinos for Latinos. The biggest problem, he pointed out, was that "there were really no Latin parts because the writers weren't Hispanic. The filmmakers weren't Hispanic. And if some clever writer decided to put a Hispanic character in, he would get questioned. 'Why are you doing that? Isn't that going to affect our box office if people think it's a Hispanic film?' It had never been done successfully before so nobody wanted to take the risk and try something new."

Rodriguez then befriended Ricardo Montalban and saw what he was accomplishing with Nosotros to improve the image of Latinos in theater and film. Thereafter, the director drew a line in the sand and decided to start casting Latinos and create his own star system: "I had to demand it and make it a personal issue. It has to be Hispanic or I won't make the film. And they let me do it that way. I had to actually go shoot a whole other movie with Salma Hayek to show work that she had done in English. I went and shot a cable movie with her before *Desperado*." That wasn't all. They still weren't convinced and so he had to shoot a screen test. "And when the dailies came in, they were like, 'Oh my God, she's amazing.'"

Rodriguez's advice: "You have to just do it. And then when they see it, they go, 'Oh, okay. Now we can imitate that.' I kept using the same actors over and over. Salma. Antonio Banderas. Cheech Marin. Building up Danny Trejo. I had to create my own star system so that when I'd go to make my next movie, I could cast the people from the previous movie and they would already be bankable because they've already been in something. You just had to break through."

The fight paid off. Rodriguez recalled, "When *Spy Kids* became the number one movie for five weeks in a row, it suddenly put all that to rest. And then anyone who wanted to try it could always point to *Spy Kids* and say, 'Oh, look, it worked there.' It played to all audiences. This made a huge difference. The ripple effects are enormous. Many people have come up to me and said, 'You changed my kid's future,' when they saw little Hispanic kids like them on the screen. And then my son saw the credits and it said, 'Written and directed by Rodriguez.' He said, 'Wow, that's like me.' Because that's his last name."

Those ripple effects are the result of individual breakthroughs that made those of other people possible. For his role in *The Godfather Part III*, Andy Garcia received a 1990 Oscar nomination for Best Supporting Actor—the first nomination for a Latino in that category in thirty-four years, since Anthony Quinn's two wins in the 1950s. Finally, in 2000, Benicio del Toro did break through and win the Best Supporting Actor Oscar for his role in *Traffic*. A year later, after her portrayal of Mexican painter Frida Kahlo, Salma Hayek was nominated for an Academy Award for Best Actress. In 2011, when Mexican actor Demián Bichir was nominated for Best Actor for his performance in *A Better Life*, it was the first nomination for a Latino since Anthony Quinn's 1964 nomination for *Zorba the Greek*. In 2013, fifty-two years since Rita Moreno won the Best Supporting Actress Award, the Mexican-born Kenyan actress Lupita Nyong'o would win in that category for her performance in *12 Years a Slave*.

Why all these milestones matter is because they are signals to Latinos in other endeavors that the breakthroughs *can* happen.

Fortunately, and I'll be the first to say it, for Latinos there is never a short supply of the stamina and work ethic required to have that breakthrough. Maybe it's because of the *we try harder* mentality that's real with most immigrant groups and with individuals not part of the mainstream. Whatever it is, I saw it over and over with artists who made a difference to the Latin Explosion and whose careers were going places never visited before.

This move toward the American mainstream met a musical crossover in 2001.

The voice of Shakira. You could say that Shakira was a crossover long before she hit the Latin and pop charts. She was born a crossover. Her voice even reflects the soul that was in her DNA as the daughter of parents from Lebanon who immigrated to Barranquilla, Colombia, where she grew up.

When her father took her to a Middle Eastern restaurant for the first time when she was four, Shakira heard the *doumbek*, the Arabic drum that accompanies belly dancing, and she instinctively began to sway back and forth at the table. So at the start there was the Middle Eastern vibe, plus the Spanish language.

There were also challenges. Shakira never forgot the music teacher who rejected her from the second-grade choir and told Shakira her voice sounded like a goat's. Then, when she was eight, Shakira's father's business went bankrupt and she was sent with her mother to Los Angeles for a while. When they returned, Shakira was shocked to discover that her father had been forced to sell all the furniture in her home, their television, and both cars. Their misfortune was put into perspective when her parents took her to a park where orphans with nothing and nowhere to go were sniffing glue to ease their pain. The financial fall and the image of the kids in that park would never leave her mind. Not many years later, at age eighteen, Shakira would establish her foundation that is dedicated to improvements in health care, nutrition, and education for impoverished children in Colombia, Latin America, and other places in the world.

Along with those cultural and emotional influences, Shakira would say that her musical awakening happened at age twelve when she heard the guitar solo in Depeche Mode's "Enjoy the Silence." That was her connection to the power in the electric guitar—from an English electronic band.

Add it up and you had a belly-dancing *rockera* who'd begun to read at age three, was writing poetry at age eight and composing lyrics and music by ten, with a vision to make life better for others. It's no wonder Sony signed her at thirteen.

Her first album in Spanish sold little more than a thousand copies, but Sofía Vergara, who is five years older than Shakira and who also grew up in Barranquilla, distinctly remembers hearing the uniqueness of Shakira's voice in those early songs. Ricky Martin noticed too when he voted to give Shakira top prize at a talent competition in Chile—though she ultimately didn't win on that stage.

And even though her first two albums had not done well commercially, I knew Shakira was on the verge of a major breakthrough, especially after she did have a hit in 1995 with *Pies Descalzos* and the song "Estoy Aquí." Her next album was going to be the ticket but it was almost taken away from her when the lyrics of the songs she was writing were stolen in an airport. She soldiered on and had the help of Gloria and Emilio.

There was a discussion about including songs in English on this album, but Gloria argued against it, saying it was not wise to stop halfway. The crossover to English would have to come later when Shakira was completely prepared. So this album would be called *Dónde Están Los Ladrones? (Where Are the Thieves?)*.

Following the lift given by the previous album, *Dónde Están Los Ladrones?* was a sensation, establishing Shakira as a big star in the Latin market. That's when it was clear to me that her success would multiply exponentially as soon as she learned to write and sing in English.

When I met her at the Palladium on Fourteenth Street in New York, I immediately told her what Sony could do for her worldwide if she learned to sing in English. There was no hesitancy at all on her part. She had a huge appetite, eyes on the prize, and at a young age had gotten great guidance from Gloria and Emilio Estefan.

But it couldn't have been easy for her, and I'll tell you why. The same girl I met at the Palladium so eager to please would later show up in my office as a headstrong woman with a yellow legal pad filled with notes that she wanted to discuss point by point—the sure sign of a perfectionist. Shakira wasn't going to take such a big leap until she was good and ready.

She had the right approach, learning English through the pages of *Leaves of Grass* by Walt Whitman and other rhyming poetry. She studied so intensely that when it came time to write in the new language she had something much greater than fluency. The new language flowed through her not in clichés from language tapes, but as poetry straight from her heart and mind in words and phrases that not many who are born speaking English would think of stitching together. Her descriptions and imagery seduced the world.

All you have to do is listen to the lyrics and music of "Whenever,

Wherever." It's everything: infectious Latin rhythms, rich instrumentation and sounds of the ancient Andes pop, plus a melody and a vocal that didn't stop until it circled the world.

Shakira never wanted to fit in any box either. She has said, "My songs don't belong to a certain place. They are not typically Colombian or typically American or typically Middle Eastern. As an artist I'm always trying to experiment, find new sounds, a fusion of elements that seem foreign but that can coexist together."

"Whenever, Wherever" was a runaway hit, and the album it was on, *Laundry Service*, sold fifteen million copies worldwide. It was executive produced by Emilio, along with Gloria putting a lot of attention into it too. After its release in the summer of 2001, Shakira hit the road, singing and belly dancing into the hearts of concertgoers everywhere.

The next album, *Oral Fixation*, was released first in Spanish, and then in English. On that release, the single "Hips Don't Lie" featuring Wyclef Jean would leave an unforgettable imprint on pop culture. The single went to number one in fifty-five countries. It was the number one song of the decade. *The decade.*

It didn't seem to matter what language she was singing in. Shakira had everybody's complete attention.

And the crossovers just kept on coming.

Not just in music but in every other way that Latinos and Latin culture could find their way into hearts and hips. Say, for instance, that you are a Colombian dance fitness guy and you've moved to the United States around the same time that Shakira is learning English to make her crossover, and you come up with a brand for your Latin-flavored approach to working out and you call it something crazy like "Zumba."

Maybe you know his name. Maybe you don't. But you've probably heard of Zumba. More than 14 million people have now that it's in 200,000 locations and 185 countries around the world.

Zumba came out of nowhere. It was an accident, really, and it shows the potential of one man and a creative idea and the interest by and for all things Latino. Truly a great entrepreneurial story, Zumba represents just the opening bars of all the Latino entrepreneurial success stories we're going to be seeing and hearing about in the future.

That's not my opinion. There is simply no debate about this. The numbers guarantee it. The number of Latino entrepreneurs in the United States is growing at a rate that is *ten* times faster than that of the overall US population. That's why a look back at how Zumba came about is really, in ways both large and small, a look at the future.

For Beto Perez, it started in Cali, Colombia, where he was working three jobs to support his family. He loved to dance, but couldn't afford lessons. He won a competition and was offered a spot in a dance academy in exchange for teaching step aerobics. One day, he forgot the tapes that he normally used to accompany his class and he improvised with salsa and merengue. Everybody loved it, and before long he opted to move to Miami to try to bring his unique style of exercise to America.

Beto Perez couldn't speak English, but he showed up one afternoon at an empty gym and the manager said: "Just teach *me*." Beto got the music going, started through the paces, and people who were coming through the front door stopped in to watch and immediately enrolled. Once he had built up a devoted following in Miami's Latino and multicultural community, Beto was approached by two entrepreneurs with the idea of expanding the company and turning it into a worldwide brand. The concept was launched with an infomercial and became an overnight success. Using follow-along choreography, the program incorporates current and older music from Latino artists and moves that come from salsa, mambo, hip-hop/reggaeton, merengue, samba, and more.

For the past fifteen years, Zumba classes have continued to pack fitness clubs and gyms, and haven't appeared to be slowing whatsoever. Why should they? For those who can't make it to the clubs but want to shake their hips and have fun while burning calories and toning up—thanks to the squats, lunges, and core exercises—Zumba gets the job done.

From music to movies to dance, it was only a hop and a skip over to food—where the *fusionistas* were soon breaking rules and pushing Latin influences to the most creative lengths. Food critics all of a sudden found new fascination in the origins of Latino cuisine and looked again, tracing them back to Spain, in turn hailing the Spaniard Ferran Adrià as the best living chef on the planet. At El Bulli, his mountaintop restaurant in Spain, Adrià invented a dish called "Kellogg's paella" that featured Rice Krispies, shrimp heads, and vanilla-flavored mashed potatoes. How's that for a culinary definition of crossover?

On Miami Beach and in New York City, the Cuban chef Douglas Rodriguez became known as the Mambo King of New Cuisine when he wrapped mussels in banana leaves, invented cappuccino egg creams, and paired foie gras with dried cherry and shallot mojo.

It was only natural that the same Americans who were turned on to Latino culture by Ricky Martin's music would become curious about Latin cuisine. They saw Ricky in interviews talking up the lobster and plantains coming out of the kitchen of his restaurant in Miami Beach. Many musicians jumped in with restaurants of their own. Gloria and Emilio started Bongos in South Beach. Jennifer Lopez opened Madre's in Pasadena. And Carlos Santana collaborated with Chef Roberto Santibañez to open five restaurants called Maria Maria—named after the song.

Over the last few decades, Latino restaurants have opened all over the United States with offerings in every demographic. After all, for immigrant entrepreneurs who can cook, serving up good food just like in the old country (wherever it happened to be) will always be welcome. And if you can sell to fellow immigrants, you have your niche market.

You might not have guessed that great Mexican food could be found in Durham, North Carolina. That may not have been true during the late nineties when there were only about two thousand Latinos living in the area—when landlords wouldn't rent space for a restaurant to Roselia Flores. The Mexican immigrant had to figure out how to buy her own land. Now Durham's Latino population is thirty-six thousand—comprising roughly 14 percent of the city's residents—and Flores owns a restaurant and a thriving supermarket. Mom-and-pop places like these have been popping up all over America.

What few people realized for many years was how long Latinos have felt at home in the US as entrepreneurs. They had no choice. When inroads to high-level professions or positions within corporate America were blocked, one of the few openings for gaining a foothold in the new culture was often the oldest road: food. Even when immigration policies for Mexicans have vacillated insanely—opening the doors in one period to come and fill spots in the labor force and then slamming them shut during times of unemployment—the nation has never wavered on the food. Americans have long had a love affair with Mexican food.

El Charro Café in Tucson is the oldest Mexican restaurant known for being continually run by the same family in the United States—it goes back to 1922. And the stove that was used at the opening of the original El Cholo in 1927 is now on display in the lobby of that restaurant in Santa Monica, California. Restaurants don't stick around for almost a century if *generations* of people don't love them.

Then there is the food success story of Maria de Lourdes Sobrino, who came to the United States from Mexico in 1982 after her travel agency business couldn't survive the devaluation of the peso. Once she had gotten settled here she looked for her favorite snack on the shelves of American grocery stores, but couldn't find it. So she decided to make some ready-to-eat parfait gelatin herself. Figuring that others might want some too, she used her mother's recipe, and began to produce three hundred cups a day, offering them to stores to sell on consignment. The product was made quickly and conveniently, was priced right, and tasted good.

That business approach, according to filmmaker and entrepreneur Robert Rodriguez, was summed up in how he was raised. "We used to say, 'Fast, cheap, or good. Pick two.' But, with Latinos, you don't have any choice; it's got to be fast, cheap, and good. You've got to be all three. And you've got to be like that all the time."

That mind-set panned out well for Lourdes' dessert company, which took on her nickname, Lulu. Her success rose to the attention of President George Bush 43, who invited her to speak at an economic forum; Microsoft shared her business smarts at one of its summits. Lulu's Dessert Corporation now sells sixty *million* cups of gelatin, *dulce de leche*, flan, and rice pudding every year. In virtually no time, Lulu went from her immigrant kitchen to the shelves of Walmart.

In all these trends, I should point out that in addition to Latino chefs and food entrepreneurs making inroads in every region of the country, non-Latinos have long embraced aspects of the culture and have taken those concepts mass market.

There are some people who might see this as a rip-off of Latino culture. But not Graciela Eleta, a strategic brand adviser born in Panama who has worked in the Latino market for decades. She sees it as a form of respect. Graciela says, "Every time I see major marketers in the US adopt flavors or spices or tortillas, it's an acceptance of our culture. It gives us a richer culture overall because it gives us a source of pride, how we in America are learning to live in a multicultural society, and learning how to be more open, tolerant, and embracing of these cultural influences."

This fusion of Latin concept and American taste buds can now be seen vividly in the megachain that is Chipotle (which was partly owned by McDonald's), and in food purveyors like El Pollo Loco, Green Burrito, Qdoba Mexican Eats, Pancheros Mexican Grill, Chili's, and McDonald's itself, which began to incorporate Latin tastes into its own menu with innovations like the McWrap.

Think about that. The McWrap. You know what the McWrap is? A sandwich in a tortilla. And they're serving mango pineapple smoothies—a tropical beverage—to wash it down.

Salsa is practically a staple in many American homes, on the way to becoming more popular than ketchup.

Add it up and you see where this was all going. It's logical that culinary superstars like César Ramirez would set up Chef's Table at Brooklyn Fare and that Ricardo Zarate would bring his Peruvian-inspired magic to restaurants in Los Angeles. But what I'm talking about goes way beyond New York, Los Angeles, and San Antonio. Aarón Sánchez has branched out with Mestizo in Kansas City, a line of home products sold at T.J. Maxx and Marshalls, as well as a Spanish-language food travel series. While Anthony Lamas' Seviche in Louisville is a must-stop on any foodie's road map.

It's now so common to find a Brazilian *churrascaria* serving *rodizio* in major cities that Fogo de Chão has twenty-five locations around the country. And that's by no means the only Brazilian steak house. If you ask Google to list the fifteen best Brazilian steak houses in the US, a story will pop up with a definitive answer.

Meanwhile, Goya has become an all-American powerhouse company, invited to *La Casablanca* to partner with First Lady Michelle Obama on a campaign to promote portion control called My Plate, *Mi Plato*. There are now sixteen Goya facilities throughout the US, Puerto Rico, the Dominican Republic, and Spain, with four thousand employees . . . and these numbers are really a sign of the growth to come as the Latino population moves from 18 percent now to more than 30 percent a generation down the road.

You can only imagine the expression on Don Prudencio's face if he could have been fast-forwarded from the day he opened that small shop on Duane Street all those years ago to being taken on a tour of the quarter-of-a-billion-dollar warehouses and offices his grandchildren are currently opening in Houston, Atlanta, Southern California, and New Jersey. All thanks to the beans.

The Latin Explosion was driven by the music, buoyed by movies and dance, and accompanied by great food and drink. After that, everything else would follow.

CHAPTER ELEVEN

Modern Family

If you can change six lives in your life, and make it better for other people, make it less painful, then you've accomplished something really big.

—EMILIO ESTEFAN

It probably can't be emphasized enough that none of the growth and expansion of opportunities for Latinos would have happened if there had not been someone long ago to lay the groundwork and someone else's footsteps to follow in. That said, it's striking that when *Spy Kids* went crazy at the box office in 2001, there had not been a Latino actor to make an impact on television since Freddie Prinze inspired George Lopez on *Chico and the Man* in the mid-seventies. That's a quarter of a century.

Not surprisingly, it turns out that the same roadblocks that existed in the film industry were in force in network television. There had been a couple of attempts at Latino-themed shows over the decades. In the eighties, the sitcom king Norman Lear tried to do a Mexican-American *All in the Family* by giving voice to comedian Paul Rodriguez and an ensemble of Latino actors that included Hector Elizondo. The show was *a.k.a. Pablo*. Biting and ahead of its time, the sitcom didn't work. Middle America didn't go for the humor. Jokes comparing "a Mexican credit card" to a "gun between the teeth" were too downscale. And Latinos were left wondering why the show was making fun of Mexicans. It was canceled after seven episodes.

FOX took a shot in the mid-nineties with John Leguizamo, but *House of Buggin'* was also halted before the end of the first season due to low ratings. Per usual, the numbers made it difficult for executives to go out on a limb to green-light new attempts. It's not easy to create a hit show of any kind. So executives had always seen taking a chance on a Latino sitcom as all risk without any realistic upside.

My sense is that what shook up that attitude was Ricky Martin's Grammy performance on national television. I think it was then that a lot of people started to sit up and wonder, Hey, why not? Why not look for ways to feature Latinos in entertaining formats that might really work on the small screen?

At this same time you had a couple of other crosscurrents taking place. On the one hand, you had Latino groups calling for a national boycott of all the major networks to protest the lack of brown faces on television; and on the other, you also had one of the biggest box office actresses, Sandra Bullock, startled that there wasn't a single Latino or Asian show on any network, deciding to make a difference for others. She began by searching comedy clubs for new and diverse talent. Her business partner, coincidentally, was

Jonathon Komack Martin—the son of the guy who'd created *Chico and the Man*. And the two of them were blown away when they saw George Lopez work onstage.

They got behind George, cut through a lot of red tape, and convinced ABC to spring for a pilot. It went well, and ABC green-lighted the series, debuting *The George Lopez Show* in 2002, opening up America to a sitcom set in the home of a Mexican-American family.

George had been raised, for the most part, by his grandmother, whom he says never once expressed pride in him. It was this relationship that George mined and exploited on his show, as a man trying to raise a family in the best way he knew how while also attempting to comically squeeze a drop of praise for his efforts from the character represented as his mother . . . who comically refused to give it to him.

The show was a reversal of casting practices that went back to *West Side Story*. Whereas all of the leading Puerto Rican characters in that movie were played by outsiders except for Rita Moreno, the actors who were cast as leads in George's show were all Latino—with the exception of Masiela Lusha, an Albanian who played George's daughter. The Mexican-American family values came across as universal working-class family values—enough to be embraced by an increasingly diverse mainstream audience. For a time, *The George Lopez Show* became the top-rated sitcom on ABC.

George understood the stakes and what they meant to others too. He made it real for himself on the set, as he explained: "There's a piece of wood that I hung in the house. It says, 'Remember, We're Making History.' I wrote it in a brown Sharpie in 2002. And I would always touch it before every show. Other people would look at it and it didn't mean anything to them. But it did to me. We were making history because *The George Lopez Show* is the only show with a Mexican-American lead in the history of TV that's ever been syndicated. That means a lot."

The George Lopez Show ran for five years—about as long as *I Love Lucy*. Of course, television shows never last forever. But once you enter through the gates of syndication heaven, that's validation of having made it. And meanwhile, opportunities were multiplying substantially as changes in TV programming cried out for more diverse talent that spoke to more diverse audiences.

We were a long way from the days when Latinos in America and pop culture were made to feel invisible. Just as George Lopez's show put a Mexican-American family front and center, linking to mainstream audiences who had the same family issues, programming for younger audiences provided springboards for rising Latin talent.

A couple of kids named Selena Gomez and Demi Lovato got parts on the children's show *Barney & Friends*. And it quickly became clear how even tiny opportunities like these could lead to major advances. Selena graduated to a small role on Disney's *Hannah Montana* and then the lead in *Wizards of Waverly Place*. Demi went on to be a star on Disney's *Sonny with a Chance* and was featured in adolescent movies like *Camp Rock*. Of course, for anyone who follows pop culture, it's unbelievable how much Selena Gomez's off-and-on relationship with Justin Bieber has kept her in the public eye, a cultural figure no matter what.

Both Gomez and Lovato would use these acting successes to launch and develop musical, marketing, and entrepreneurial crossovers. It's clear to me that Latinas who have come of age and achieved prominence on television have been empowered not only to ride their wave of success but to really use their clout as far as they can go, as entrepreneurs and philanthropists too. Eva Longoria is a great example of an actress who has leveraged her achievements in television to become a real player in entertainment—as an actress and producer determined to create opportunities for other Latinos, and as a leader who wants to see her community do more to flex its muscle at the ballot box.

Eva, from Corpus Christi, Texas, who grew up being inspired by her homegirl Selena, never forgot what it was like to witness a female Tejano singer expanding her ambitions to open a clothing salon and start her own fashion line. In this respect, there are many, like Eva Longoria, who can point to Selena as the trailblazer and ultimate role model for Latina empowerment.

In fact, marketers at Telemundo, the Spanish-language television network (a subsidiary of NBCUniversal), went so far as to identify the rising influence and common traits of Latinas between eighteen and thirty-four, an increasingly important demographic. At Telemundo they give this group a name: the Modern Independent Achievers. Or the MIAs.

Jacqueline Hernández, chief operating officer of Telemundo,

noted that Selena was one of the first modern-day MIAs, describing what those traits were: "A singer. A businesswoman. Proud. Confident. That's the essence of the MIA. While at the same time, she's all about her family. The MIAs are the next generation of Latinas—and they want it all. They want the corner office, the home, and the kids; they want to be there with their parents and their grandparents and have the Prada bag. I have MIAs who work in my office. I see the MIAs every day. And down the road you're going to be seeing more and more of them."

In stark contrast to the older, restrictive, traditional values that discouraged Latinas from seeking careers outside of the home, the Modern Independent Achiever has other priorities:

- The value of education, and the use of it to get ahead.
- An ambicultural point of view.
- Independence that can cross over to rebellion.
- An attachment to and respect for family that can offset what appears to be disobedience.
- And the desire to evolve beyond traditional barriers.

As an MIA all the way, Eva Longoria finished her college degree before pursuing her acting career, first by breaking into soaps and then by becoming a household name as the sizzling Gabrielle Solis on the ABC television series *Desperate Housewives*. Actually, before leaving Texas, Eva got her feet wet when the movie *Selena* was being shot. She even waited on line for hours just to be an extra in one scene. To give you an idea how much things had changed in such a short span of time, when Eva arrived in Hollywood it was not long after Ricky Martin's "La Copa de la Vida" performance at the Grammys and the wave of activism demanding more diversity in TV. The timing was good. Instead of finding there were no parts for Latinas, she arrived at a moment when that was changing.

"People told me, 'Oh great. There's this Latin Explosion happening,'" Eva recalled. "Ricky Martin was exploding. Selena's music had crossed over. And Jennifer Lopez was becoming a big thing. And I thought, awesome. I guess I'm Latino." Then she learned the reality of what Hollywood thought was Latino. Eva said, "I remember going in to an audition and them asking me to do an accent. And I was like, an accent of what? I didn't understand. I don't even know anybody who has an accent in my family. So, all of a sudden, I wasn't Latin enough. That was a big awakening. Everybody sees me as Latin, but I'm just totally American."

To put a finer point on it, Eva grew up as a ninth-generation Texan whose ancestors had lived under six flags without moving, and though she was Mexican-American she spoke no Spanish at the time. The Latino roles played by her and Ricardo Antonio Chavira, the actor who played Gabrielle's husband on *Desperate Housewives*, were a new way for America to see Latinos. They were the wealthiest couple on the block—and their *gardener* was *white*. Lupe Ontiveros, the Mexican-American actress who'd played a maid more than a hundred times throughout her career, was no longer the maid. She was the *mother-in-law* of the wealthiest woman on the block.

Desperate Housewives, a satiric, sexy prime-time soap, broke all the rules, and probably laid down the gauntlet for such other prime-time soaps as *Scandal* and *How to Get Away with Murder*, not to mention the various shows with the "real housewives" of reality TV.

Not only that, but with the popularity of Eva's character and her Latino family on *Desperate Housewives*, ABC was emboldened to adapt a successful Latin telenovela—*Yo Soy Betty, La Fea*, a modern-day story of how the ugly duckling becomes the swan—to American tastes. The Mexican-born Salma Hayek was *Ugly Betty's* executive producer. A Cuban-American, Silvio Horta, directed it. And the TV series turned a Honduran-American actress, America Ferrera, into a star.

The world was shifting. With so much growing competition on cable and subscription TV and on streaming platforms, network executives were now in a place where they needed to reach out to younger, more diverse audiences—including those who were watching Spanish-speaking networks, like Univision and Telemundo. The average age of Univision's audience in prime time is now thirty-seven, as opposed to fifty-five for the English-speaking viewers of mainstream network television.

When it came to Latino viewership, the sweetest spot that show creators and advertisers needed to hit was now the bilingual cross-over market. True, some Latinos speak no English, about 20 percent; some speak no Spanish, about 20 percent also. But 60 percent of Latinos speak both. That's why *Ugly Betty* in English worked so well—because it was content that had the potential of capturing 80 percent, or the lion's share of Latinos, who were bilingual or only spoke English.

In almost no time, the Latin Explosion had crossed over to

television and was quietly permeating content in a variety of genres, for all kinds of viewers. Some didn't even need to have accents and some had them in a big way.

When the creators of *Modern Family* set out to refresh and revisit the classic family sitcom, they wisely incorporated the new reality of blended families that are becoming more and more prevalent. Most families have members who are in second or third marriages. Many families have members who marry someone who doesn't come from the same racial, cultural, or religious background as they do. Many families have members who are LGBT and are in committed relationships, if not marriages, and who are raising children together. So in *Modern Family*, which uses the faux documentary style, you have some of those dynamics and get to watch all the complications, humor, dysfunction, and resolution in the relationships between ten very different people in three entirely different households all bonded by the connection that is family.

Not every demographic is represented on *Modern Family* but the show's creators definitely crafted a career-making role for a Latina played by Sofía Vergara.

Sofía had first been spotted on a beach in Colombia by an agent when she was seventeen, and she soon booked a Pepsi commercial that had her peeling down to a bikini while stepping on hot sand on her way to buying her cold drink. Along the way, every guy on the beach is following her progress, including the lifeguard. Nobody has stopped looking at Sofía since.

She arrived in Miami in the nineties and worked on a popular travel show on Univision, *Fuera de Serie*, that took her to exotic spots around the world, made her a star in the Latin-American market, and also gave her exposure in the US.

But that looked to be her ceiling; finding the right fit in the American market was tough because of her accent. When she took "accent" lessons to try to speak more like an American she found it inhibited her as an actress. That changed in 2009, thanks to *Modern Family*, Sofía claimed, because they wrote the character for her. She emphasized the fact that "the creators tried to educate themselves in how a Latin woman was, how she looked, and they let me embrace all of those things and bring a lot of my real life and my Latin personality into the scenes."

The character of Gloria Delgado also allowed Sofía to access her mother and her aunt in a way that is somehow reminiscent of what Desi Arnaz was able to achieve in *I Love Lucy*. While some critics have complained that her character is more of a caricature, I have to say that *every* character on that show is a bit of a caricature. The genius in the faux documentary style is that it pushes the comedy envelope without going completely over the top.

As the father of four—two older kids from my first marriage to their Jewish mother (I converted at the time) and two younger kids who are part Mexican (you could say I converted to Latino)—I know a lot about blended families. On *Modern Family*, the younger characters always have me howling—like Manny, the son of Sofía's character on the show.

There's a great story about the casting of Manny that begins with another Latino family from Bryan, Texas, and goes back to the mid-1980s when two nineteen-year-old newlyweds, Roy and Diane, were thinking about how to get ahead and achieve some security.

Diane was working at night for a phone company. Roy wanted to make a career in air-conditioning and refrigeration, but there was no school for that nearby. So Roy began driving his Chevy pickup about an hour and a half every weekday from Bryan to Houston to take the course. One day, Roy realized he had a bad tire and noticed a fenced cage filled with used tires at a tire shop that had just been built on the outskirts of Houston.

The owner of the shop said the tires were going to be carted away, and explained that the shop had to pay for their disposal. When Roy asked him if he could have a single tire, the owner said: "If you want one, you'd have to take them all."

Roy didn't have to think too long. He stacked about seventy-five tires in his pickup, drove them back to Bryan, and set them in the backyard of his mobile home. Soon, he and his wife were hocking their wedding rings, watches, and jewelry to get their own tire store going. Thirty days later, they had done enough business to get their jewelry back from the pawnshop.

When the economy took a dive, Roy and Diane lost their home, but managed to start another tire shop, where they decided to live instead of paying rent. Roy noticed a concrete-block building getting knocked down nearby, found out he could take the blocks for free, and used them to build a tiny apartment inside the store.

Diane and their kids all worked in the shop. One day, their

daughter, Raini, read an article about a talent audition for actors at a local hotel, and asked her parents if she could go. Because she had been helping out in customer service, Raini had actually honed her acting skills and nailed the audition. The result? Raini Rodriguez is now one of the stars of the Disney sitcom *Austin & Ally*. And the story doesn't end there. When Raini's mom took her out to California to pursue an acting career, she also took Raini's younger brother, Rico.

You may have guessed it. That would be the same Rico Rodriguez who would ultimately get the part of Manny on *Modern Family*. It's safe to say that the modern Latino family is moving on up with a lot of mom-and-pop entrepreneurs who are raising Modern Independent Achievers, both male and female—whether as singers, dancers, and actors, or doctors and lawyers and major players in corporate America.

Those ideals have always been American values, just as *Modern Family* shares values in a comedy form that everybody can relate to. No question. The sitcom's message of inclusion has touched a nerve in pop culture, winning multiple Emmy Awards year in and year out. Almost thirteen million people a week tune in to watch *Modern Family*. And, yep, as more evidence of how far the Latin Explosion has gone, Sofía is now the highest-paid actress on television.

Meanwhile, advertisers have jumped on the bandwagon with generous endorsement deals for Latinas, who represent a new American beauty image. Diversity has become an advantage in every way. Sofía Vergara has a beauty campaign for CoverGirl that includes filming commercials with Ellen DeGeneres. For CoverGirl, they can target the mainstream and multicultural, diverse audiences. For a Latina with a homegrown accent, that's the *Modern Family* version of all-American. Similarly, L'Oréal reaches a wider array of consumers when it showcases Eva Longoria—an example of how one star can galvanize more than one market, and another aspect of the fusion that started with music and has taken hold of TV.

It's happening in ways we don't really know. When nearly six million kids tuned in to the premiere of *Victorious* on Nickelodeon, most weren't aware that actress Victoria Justice has Puerto Rican roots. The kids simply tuned in to Victoria Justice. When you think back on how Rita Moreno as a child had no Latina role models, that makes it pretty cool to see the presence of young Latinas like Victoria Justice, Selena Gomez, Demi Lovato, and even the cartoon character Dora the Explorer.

We've gotten to the point where new shows like *Jane the Virgin*, adapted from a Venezuelan telenovela, and the sitcom *Cristela*, created by the stand-up comedienne Cristela Alonzo, no longer will be judged and commented upon as novelties. If they win Golden Globes, like Gina Rodriguez did for her work in *Jane the Virgin*, they will be successful. If they don't bring in numbers, like *Cristela*, they will go the way of every other show with poor ratings.

What else is new, right? But wait.

Something is new. What entrepreneurial Latinos in the entertainment industry are saying is, why should they be beholden to or dependent on mainstream producers to develop and broadcast content that may or may not be relevant or authentic? With fifty million Latinos now in the United States and nearly 80 percent of them speaking English, why can't Latinos play a more prominent role in seeing *more* of their talent and stories on-screen?

The answer, for Eva Longoria, is UnbeliEVAble Entertainment, her production company, which has multiple projects shooting for both the big screen and the small screen. For Sofía Vergara, the answer is LatinWE, which has been called the leading Latino talent and marketing agency in the United States. For director Robert Rodriguez, it is creating and launching El Rey, a cable network aimed at galvanizing Latino and mainstream viewing habits across the country.

Rodriguez put it this way: "When this idea of this television network came up, I thought, 'Wow! That's a huge-sized nut to take on, to run a network, and create programming for it. That's a beast.' But my hand shot up immediately. I have five kids. Even though they're bilingual, they mostly live and converse in English. And there's nothing on television that represents who they are. So I wanted to change that for them and for everybody who needs that reassurance that they exist in this country."

Jennifer Lopez has also raised her hand.

It's been incredible to watch her evolve and play a leading role in the Latin Explosion, pushing past the borders of music and acting, into television and film production, into clothing lines and top-selling fragrances. When late-night television host David Letterman read off a list of all the perfumes Jennifer had released, it seemed to go on for five hilarious minutes. Her understanding of the new sound of America was apparent during her tenure in a judge's seat on *American Idol*. Between her clothing line with Kohl's and Tommy Hilfiger, plus a home collection, as well as endorsing the Fiat 500 Cabrio by driving it through the old neighborhood in a commercial, she has become a very savvy entrepreneur. Her films to date have grossed more than two billion dollars, and a few years back *Forbes* magazine wrote that she might be the most powerful entertainer on the planet.

Around that time, Jenny from the Block went into partnership with NuvoTV, a cable TV outlet for Latinos that has a goal of lifting its audience by showing viewers more of themselves on television. Jennifer has explained her intention by saying:

> If I was inspired by just one movie like *West Side Story* and one actress like Rita Moreno—and that's all I needed to see in order to go out and do what I did—imagine what will happen when people can see themselves through programming twenty-four hours a day, seven days a week. Imagine what that's going to inspire. Imagine how many more Latinos are going to feel, "Maybe I should try that . . ." Maybe it will inspire them to get out and reach their full potential.

All of these endeavors speak to what Emilio Estefan means when he says that if you can change six lives in your life, and make it better for other people, then you've accomplished something really big. That pretty much sums up what I think modern family values should be, values that I think are in the DNA of Latinos who care about lifting all families to attain their potential.

However, it's one thing to have the muscle to do that. It's another to flex it. That's a message that started to come through loud and clear from a Cuban-American guy from Miami by the name of Armando Christian Pérez.

CHAPTER TWELVE

Mr. Worldwide

In some of these board meetings with major companies, I'll be asked, "How do we infiltrate your culture?" I say, "*Infiltrate?* Jesus, I didn't know I had to bring an AK-47 to this meeting, man." How do we even use these kinds of words? So in a case like this the responsibility for me is to protect us, and make sure that when they do show the world who we are, they're not degrading, diluting, or stereotyping where we're from, what we do, and how we do it.

—PITBULL

Let's rewind briefly to the year 2002. That was when two forces majeures clashed right at the same time. It was the turning point when the entire distribution model for selling recorded music was stood on its head, which in turn set off the avalanche that would swallow up the whole music industry as we knew it. It was also when the seemingly unstoppable rise of the Latin Explosion hit its peak.

Many artists who used to be able to support themselves through album sales no longer could. Their one or two most popular songs on an album were being cherry-picked by consumers for less than one dollar apiece, downloaded through iTunes, and very little of that revenue was trickling down to them.

The music companies were shaken by the loss of their share of

CD sales at stores like Tower Records, and they no longer had the same resources to put into promoting these artists. Not long down the road, YouTube would be invented and anybody with a computer could see artists performing their greatest hits for free. Next thing you knew, everybody had a smartphone. Suddenly, you could watch your favorite artists singing your favorite songs in the palm of your hand. Whenever you wanted. For free.

A new model needed to be created to support the artists in this new environment. An *entrepreneurial* model. The model that emerged asked artists to derive more revenues through touring, linking up with sponsors, and collaborating with other artists to increase popularity.

Enter a kid who looked white, rapped in Spanish and English, and took on the nickname of a dog that doesn't know what it's like to lose: Pitbull. His music and persona were all about the party. That meant he was made to order for almost all millennials—the most dominant group of culture consumers ever, and an audience that every advertiser wanted to reach.

Had Pitbull arrived in an earlier era, he might have had a few hits in the party music genre and then the world might have moved on. But his unique look, his upbringing, his work ethic, and his music were magnified by the emerging power of the Latino market, as well as by the new distribution opportunities made possible by technology.

Armando Christian Pérez was born in Miami to Cuban parents in 1981—a rapper almost from the time he could put sentences together. At age three, he was reciting the words of José Martí—the poet and "Apostle of Independence" to Cubans in the nineteenth century. Armando's parents separated early in his life, and he was raised by his mother. His drug-dealing days in high school have been well documented, and he does not shy away from acknowledging them. But less commonly known is how his mother played a pivotal role in raising him to seek another path. She encouraged him to listen to every Tony Robbins motivational tape she could get her hands on. Likewise, his grandmother snuck lessons into mealtime and whenever else possible.

Pitbull's father also reminded his son of values that ultimately kept him focused. His dad would always tell him: "Don't forget where you are from and what we have gone through to be able to be in this country."

Pitbull's success was never preordained. Once it had happened, he admitted, "No one thought I'd be here. I was supposed to become something else. And I would have, if it wasn't for a great upbringing. And music." That was his way out. As he put it, "Music was my escape."

He was definitely an outlier. His blue eyes confused other Latinos in Miami who thought he was white, and they were often surprised to hear him speak Spanish. Over time, Pitbull accepted that he was different while learning how to fit in with all groups of friends—Latino, white, and black. In the world of rap and hip-hop, the ability to speak authentically in a way that could translate across a racial or cultural divide was a powerful draw.

That's apparently what producer Luther Campbell spotted in Pitbull when he decided to take him on as an artist. Campbell had been a member of 2 Live Crew, a group notorious for strip-club lyrics back in the late eighties and early nineties. He had famously been arrested on obscenity charges and had sued all the way to the Supreme Court—and won. Pushed to the margins by the mainstream music industry, Campbell thrived as a full-fledged entrepreneur, making his own music, pressing his own CDs, running his own tours, and collaborating with other artists to continually expand his audience. It was the pathway of the future, and when Pitbull signed on with Campbell, he stepped onto the right road at just the right time.

That was just how a Latino rapper who sounded black and looked white quietly entered the Wild, Wild West of the music marketplace in October 2002 when his first recorded mainstream performance was released on a solo track from Lil Jon's album *Kings of Crunk*. Another couple of years would pass before his releases conquered the music charts. But by the time that they did, his crossover sound had already invaded dance clubs, parties, and Zumba classes all around the world.

None of this success happened by accident or kismet.

The world had changed. We were now in an era of the entertainer as entrepreneur. And that is the key to how Armando Christian Pérez, aka Pitbull, aka Mr. 305, went on to become Mr. Worldwide.

This was a whole new ball game in many ways. For one thing, if you look at the rising profile of Latino consumers that had come

---

along with the Latin Explosion in music and media, you can see the heightened appeal of this empowered demographic to mainstream marketers. Making the connection hadn't always been easy for the big brands. In fact, long before Pitbull ever appeared in a Bud Light commercial, mainstream US companies had struggled in their campaigns to reach out to the Latino market.

A large segment of the marketing industry used to think that getting a mainstream brand's message across to this demographic was simply about language. They figured that the same message they put out in English could be translated into a campaign for Spanish speakers, and that the Latino audience would immediately identify with it.

They were in for a surprise. That's the point made by Arturo Nunez, head of marketing for Apple in Latin America and the Caribbean. Nunez remembered:

> When I was at Johnnie Walker Black Label, we worked on a campaign to attract a new generation of drinkers. The central question was: How do we get a new young generation of people drinking whisky when it's perceived as a drink for the wood-paneled library, the logs burning in the fireplace, the bearskin rug, and the old guy with the pipe? That was the heritage in the US.
>
> The basis of the US campaign was: "It's not just your father's drink anymore." The campaign was working. They were modernizing the persona of Johnnie Walker's whisky. Then they thought: *Hey, we just need to translate this into Spanish for*

Latinos. They were trying to target the Miami market and the Hispanics in New York.

I came to the table and said: "Hey, guys, the idea that 'it's not just your father's drink' is not going to work for Latinos." In Hispanic culture it's a rite of passage to drink what your father's drinking. It's a good thing. Not a bad thing. You're not going to win any fans by saying this is not your father's drink. The Latino generation coming up is trying to be a grown man, and a grown man drinks Johnnie Walker. The idea is for him to drink it with his dad.

They said: "Whoa! We hadn't thought about that." That's when they understood that it wasn't about translating the language. It was about translating into culture first.

Similarly, any attempts to translate a message by merely integrating a Latin musical beat weren't enough; they failed even worse when marketers relied on stereotypes and didn't respect the culture.

Luis Miguel Messianu, founder of Alma, the sixth largest Latin advertising agency in the US, recalls leaving California for Miami in the early nineties and looking for a bank to use. "I saw this commercial," he said, "where the tellers were dancing salsa. I kept thinking to myself, *Do I really want to put my money there? Those tellers sure can dance, but do they know a lot about investments?*"

The Latino audience was way too savvy to accept these stereotypes, and mainstream companies had to learn to adjust. Many are still having a hard time. But others have begun to communicate with Latinos through their strengths: family, trust, loyalty, bold flavors, passion, and tradition.

State Farm Insurance, for example, was able to battle GEICO in the Latin market by promoting the personal touch of its agents. It was an added value that catered to Latinos' sense of loyalty and trust, and enabled State Farm to position itself as a confidence company as opposed to a car insurance company. Honey Nut Cheerios broke its messaging into niche markets. The family of Latinos dancing in the kitchen with Buzz the Bee to the music of "Corazón de Melao" was a direct appeal to the joy of family and good health.

These developments are better late than not at all. As Eva Longoria has said, companies have finally woken up to the Latino buying power that's available to them, and are starting to realize, "Oh shoot, if we don't start marketing to this emerging market, we're going to actually lose profit."

George Lopez concurs, pointing out that there's a lot more work to do to appeal to Latinos. "Especially in advertising where we are the largest customers. We buy the most diapers, we buy the most beer, we buy the most cleaning products, clearly, and we pay a lot of the times in cash. We have credit cards. We love cars. We're already spending more money than we have. You would think that would be a culture that you would handle with more respect than it's being shown."

Eva Longoria reminded me that awareness of the Latino consumer is just good business. She saw it in action on a trip to Disneyland:

If you're on any of the little trams you hear many languages. You know, "Keep your hands inside the ride." Then they say it in Spanish. Then they say it in Chinese. They say it in many languages. And somebody next to me said: "That's so nice that they do that. So nice that they put the other languages in."

And I said: "*Nice? That's smart.*" They're capitalizing when everybody spends their money here.

Jennifer Lopez also addressed just how much advertisers and investors are starting to pay attention in ways they hadn't before, and why seizing the opportunity has to happen correctly:

We're in a revolution, and it's just starting. I feel that in everything that I do. I think about every project that I take on, anything that I create. I always make sure that we are depicted and are represented in the way that we exist.

Latinos have this thing of *We're just grateful for what we have and we're fine right here.* But then there's how people saw us. Like, that's the valet, and that's the cook. And that's the gardener. And, unfortunately, that was people's view of Latinos in the past . . . for many, many years, you know?

Now, because of so many different things, because of political figures, artists, performers, Latinos are coming to the forefront and saying: "Hey, we're here and we contribute." And we want to be seen. Even financially, the power that we hold in this day and age—everybody's always trying to tap into that market, you know?

And I know that's why a lot of people come to me and say, "We want the Latino dollars. How do we do this?" It's kind of crazy. We respond to what everybody else responds to. What's good—give us something good and we'll consume it. It's no big mystery.

These thoughts underscore the appeal of Pitbull for marketers, because of his proximity to the culture. Here you had a voice who rapped in English *and* Spanish, and who brought the Miami streets to the American sound track. In twenty-first-century advertising nothing could top the success of marrying a brand with a Latino music celebrity who also had the authenticity of hip-hop street cred—making him cool as well as trustworthy to consumers from all backgrounds. The messaging crossed both ways. For Latinos he could be one of them, and for everybody else, someone the whole world wanted to have at their party.

Pitbull became a bridge between cultures, no crossover required. As he quipped on *The View*, when asked if he was dating anyone at the time, "I'm single, bilingual, and ready to mingle."

Add to all of this the fact that Pitbull understood early on that *he* was the brand. Think about what's happened since he started to pile up the hits, always with his ability to be ready with a hot new release as soon as the last one was peaking. Maybe you were part of the tidal wave, dancing to songs of his like "Culo" (featuring Lil Jon) or "Ay Chico (Lengua Afuera)" or "I Know You Want Me (Calle Ocho)"—2009's smash hit that put him at the center of American culture, racking up 92 million views on YouTube alone.

Or maybe you were listening to his collaborations with every top name in hip-hop and pop, in particular with other Latino artists, like Christina Aguilera, Enrique Iglesias, Marc Anthony, Shakira, and Jennifer Lopez.

Whether you took the ride or not, no matter where you go on this earth, somehow Pitbull will reach out to you, shouting out his brand at some point in some way like an emcee on a dance floor—"Mr. Worldwide!"

He could be hosting *Pitbull's New Year's Revolution* from Miami on FOX.

Or acting in a Super Bowl ad. Or writing the theme song for the World Cup in Rio. Or showing up at an event for Walmart in Kodiak, Alaska.

Pitching a French vodka in Spanish.

Or being named the global ambassador for Playboy.

Collaborating with Ke$ha on "Timber" for a number one hit in twenty countries around the world. Or stepping to the podium at the American Music Awards.

There's a telling story that Pitball uses to explain one of his secrets to worldwide success—whether it's the way he connects with advertisers, reaches his audience by concealing an empowering message in his music, pushes the Latino vote, or uplifts the education system. That strategy, it turns out, comes from a lesson his grandmother taught him as a boy. He relates it to the mealtime conversations with his *abuela*.

"When I was younger," Pitbull remembers, "I always loved rice and steak—that was my favorite. But I didn't like to eat lettuce and tomato. So when my grandmother wanted me to eat lettuce and tomato, she'd tell me, 'Look at the lizard!' And I went to look for the lizard. 'Where's it at?' And while I was looking, she put the lettuce and tomato under the rice and the steak. And I'd eat it. After about three or four times of doing that, I was asking for the lettuce and the tomato."

What was his point and where was he going with it?

His answer: "My message is embodied through music. I'm making you dance, making you have fun, making you escape. But there's a message under there. Subliminally, I'm hitting you little by little and you don't even know it. If I were to make a record about what's happening on the border right now, nobody would care. But if I make a record that you're dancing to and enjoying yourself, but I throw in one line about what's going on at the border right now, then people start to go, 'Wait a second . . .' and they listen to it more carefully. They relate to it more. And then they're starting to get the message little by little."

For me, it was gratifying to see how Pitbull began to take entrepreneurship to a whole new level, not only when he linked himself to major brands but when he started to study the world of business and pursue opportunities for truly being an economic influencer. As someone who has always been a sponge for learning from others who were the best and most knowledgeable in their fields—what has been a mainstay in my own success—I appreciated that part of Pitbull was all about educating himself and sponging up knowledge from the leading power players in the world. He started to hang out with family members of Carlos Slim, the Mexican billionaire who is one of the wealthiest people, if not the wealthiest person, in the world.

Pitbull also figured out what many successful artists start to forget once they begin to live in rarefied air—the need to stay connected to culture. Miami was a treasure trove of musical influences coming together in grooves like reggaeton—music that brings together Latino hip-hop, Jamaican dance hall, an offshoot of Trinidadian calypso called soca, rap, and electronica. Pitbull never disconnected from that scene and continued to keep his finger on the pulse.

He was in sync with decision makers at Univision and decided to team up with Cristina on *El Show de Cristina*. She observed, "Reggaeton music had never been given the time of day before. We were the first to give this kind of music a chance." By featuring the more underground voices, the show became all the more relevant, and ratings were huge. Cristina went on. "I started mixing and matching. I noticed Pitbull was so intelligent that I let him cohost the show with me. Matches like those worked to everyone's advantage."

Pitbull wasn't just creating alliances and lucrative deals for himself. He was also shaping an entrepreneurial vision for the Latino community to become the economic force it has the potential to be. Again, the timing to do that could not have been more opportune.

In case I have hidden the message too much, I should now emphasize that the new sound of America that we've been following through the music has also become the booming sound of Latinos impacting the marketplace.

A report from the award-winning professor of economics at the University of Texas–Pan American, Alberto Dávila, assessed that the numbers of Latino entrepreneurs tripled between 1990 and 2012 and now surpass two million. Those numbers contributed to the formulation of an economic wave.

If you're one of the 140,000 Latino businesses in the New York area alone, that means you're one of every seven businesses in the city and growing.

Dávila cited the success of Eduardo Gonzalez, who came to the United States a day before the US embassy was closed in Cuba on December 29, 1960. He and his family lived frugally, and he remembers saving and saving, rarely buying anything, skimping even on furniture. He began working in the steel business in 1978, then borrowed money from his father and brother in order to bid on equipment and a lease for a company that processes flat-rolled steel. Gonzales started with five employees in 1983. Today, Ferragon Corporation in Cleveland has become a national leader in steel processing through the hustle of its immigrant workers who come from twenty-three different countries.

Success like that of Ferragon Corporation has changed the perception of Latinos in the workplace. We know the struggles of migrant Latino workers who pick grapes in California. But now we are learning about the Latino winemakers who *used to* pick grapes and *now* own their own labels. In fact, fourteen Latino winemakers in Napa and Sonoma would go on to form their own association.

That entrepreneurial spirit, no question, exists in many communities. Certainly, I saw it in my Italian-American father's drive to give his family the security and opportunity that his parents didn't have. Professor Dávila will tell you that Latinos are not inherently more disposed to entrepreneurship than any other particular group. But it is true that growing numbers of Latino immigrants fed a surge in entrepreneurship that became a wave propelled by the Latin Explosion.

Major milestones kept being reached.

In 2003, Latina entrepreneur Linda Alvarado was inducted into the National Women's Hall of Fame. After growing up in an adobe home with no indoor plumbing in New Mexico, she had worked her way through California's prestigious Pomona College as a landscaper, put down concrete sidewalks, built bus stops, and opened her own construction company—signing her name to proposals as L. Alvarado because she feared if people found out she was a woman they wouldn't do business with her. This was the start of her journey toward becoming the first Latino, male or female, to own a major-league baseball team, as the co-owner of the Colorado Rockies.

The same year that Alvarado received her Hall of Fame honor, Arte Moreno became the next Latino to own a major sports team when he bought the Anaheim Angels from the Walt Disney Company. Arte had grown up in Tucson as the oldest of eleven children. He was an entrepreneur by blood. One of his grandfathers owned Tucson's first Spanish-language newspaper and his father owned a small printshop. After fighting in the Vietnam War and graduating from the University of Arizona, Arte made his name running a billboard company that was ultimately sold for eight billion dollars.

Of course, let's not forget that Latinos in baseball have had a strong presence for decades, mostly on the field. In fact, the last time I checked, 38 percent of major-league baseball players were Latino. Recent changes in our relations with Cuba may bring that up to 50 percent or higher in a short time.

One of baseball's Latino heroes who should be mentioned in making these changes possible is Fernando Valenzuela—once a chubby kid with long hair who couldn't speak English when scouts for the Los Angeles Dodgers located him in a dot of a town in the Sonoran Desert. Fernando came to the major leagues at nineteen years old with a unique windup that corkscrewed his body and had him looking up at the sky before he delivered each pitch. Nobody had ever seen anything like him. He won his first five games of the 1981 season, four of them by shutout, then tied a major-league record by winning his first eight games straight. He also played the role of peacemaker between the Chicano community and the city of Los Angeles. After years of boycotting Chavez Ravine, where the stadium had been located, Mexican-Americans returned in record numbers to see Valenzuela pitch and then filled every opposing ballpark that he pitched in too. What made him even more iconic was the song that fans of all backgrounds sang whenever he approached the mound—"Fernando" by Abba, a Swedish pop group. "Fernandomania" swept the city and many parts of the country, bringing pride to brown, black, white, and everybody else in between. What can you say? That's the American melting pot for you.

From the time that Jackie Robinson broke down barriers for players of color, followed not many years later by Roberto Clemente doing the same for those who also had an accent, baseball has been an arena for Latino immigrants to make their careers and their fortunes—while also enriching the fans who cheer for them. You know their names: Dominican Albert Pujols, winner of the National League Most Valuable Player Award for the St. Louis Cardinals; the Yankees' Mariano Rivera, a Panamanian and the best relief pitcher in the game, who was crucial to the Yankees' World Series wins; and, also from the Dominican Republic, the Boston Red Sox's "Big Papi" Ortiz, with his larger-than-life personality and his colorful language and his big-swinging bat.

For superstar Latino athletes these days—especially those signing deals like the one Alex Rodriguez did when he signed a ten-year contract with the Texas Rangers in 2000 that was worth 250 million dollars—it's also important to be entrepreneurial.

Ten years ago it became apparent to me that you could go to almost any sporting event and run into a Latino star. Manu Ginobili became a hero not only in Argentina but in San Antonio, where he helped win four championships for the NBA's Spurs. Wide receiver Victor Cruz celebrated every touchdown pass he caught for the New York Giants with a salsa dance in honor of his Puerto Rican grandmother. Latino fighters remain the lifeblood of boxing as they have been for almost forty years, since Panama's Roberto Durán won his first of six championships. Oscar De La Hoya, an

Olympic and world champion from Los Angeles, took it to the next level by creating his own promotion company: Golden Boy.

The jockeys who compete in horse racing's Triple Crown are largely Latino. And there are Latinos of prominence in tennis, golf, mixed martial arts, women's athletics, Olympic events, and college sports. There are even Latino stars with surprisingly large followings in the multibillion-dollar surfing industry.

Imagine, one marketer recently wondered, if just one agent represented all the Latino athletes in the world. How much money do you think that *one* agent would be bringing in?

The calculations you'd make would quickly escalate here in the United States as the popularity of the game of soccer spreads even more. For many Latinos, it's the sport of choice for their kids, one of expanding opportunity for the future. A perfect example of the connection between soccer and Latino immigrants recently came out of the town of Siler City, North Carolina. After an economic downturn, the town was hit hard like many rural communities until an influx of Latino immigrants breathed new life into Siler City— first by filling jobs at poultry plants and at hatcheries created to meet demands at those plants. Next, many of the shuttered stores were brought back to life by businesses that included a vibrant *tienda*. It was only natural that the local AM station's declining ratings would then get a boost from a nightly Spanish-language show. Now nearly half of the population in Siler City is Latino and the kids of those Latino families have grown up playing soccer—to the point that their high school team, Los Jets, recently vied for the state championship, a story covered by Jennifer Lopez's new television network.

Soccer's position around the world is unprecedented. Television programming that covers soccer has become a ratings boon on English- and Spanish-language networks. And Nike now spends nearly 40 percent of its global sports endorsements on soccer—more than it spends on basketball.

The surge in soccer's appeal in this country is an economic reality that all marketers need to understand. And the influence of immigrant preferences among younger generations may also explain why Argentina's Lionel Messi tops the popularity of Dwyane Wade of the Miami Heat in a recent poll of favorite athletes among American kids.

It boggles my mind to think of how the global landscape has changed.

I can remember Shakira sitting in my office in the year 2000 as we discussed a crossover to English. Ten years later I was glued to the TV, emotionally watching her perform "Waka Waka (This Time for Africa)" at the World Cup in South Africa. She sang in English, Spanish, Fang, Zulu, and Xhosa in what would become, at one point, the most watched YouTube video of all time. It's closing in on *a billion* hits.

As the saying goes—however you choose to pronounce it—the marriage of entrepreneurship, sports, and music has been very, very good for Latinos.

What I most admire in Pitbull's approach to economic empowerment is the recognition that change doesn't happen without engaging younger Latinos and empowering them as a priority. The program he has developed for Miami's economically disadvantaged youth is called SLAM—which stands for Sports Leadership and Management—and is housed in a seven-story school. Instead of pushing math as the main criterion, Pitbull says, "We flipped the curriculum to sports, so if they're doing algebra we put the question to them like this: If X is the forty-yard line, and Y is ten seconds left, and Z is we need three points, how do we get this done?"

It's what Pitbull calls "short steps, long vision."

The results are astounding once kids are motivated, he insists.

What better than sports to teach kids that the harder you work, the better you get? What better than sports to teach them what discipline is? What better than sports to teach them what a team is? You do wrong, and everybody gets messed up. You fall together or you win together. What better than sports? Because kids love sports. We put the school in Little Havana and have kids from Allapattah, Wynwood, Liberty City, Overtown. Kids that were written off. I go into the school and see these kids; I look into their eyes and I can tell you their story. I have an idea what they're going through at home. I can imagine what their parents are going through. And it gives me goose bumps to think where these kids are going to be ten years from now. I'm going to be walking around somewhere and a kid is going to come up to me and say, "Hey, man, I ended up going to Harvard and now I'm a chemical engineer. Thank you so much for building our school."

The more people he educates in his own way, the more follow-ers he has; and the more followers he has, the more businesses he has a chance to educate.

Mr. Worldwide approaches everything he does with that same entrepreneurial drive. He strategizes and measures the kids' progress at SLAM just as he runs his own business brand. Pitbull describes his business board meetings, which are a regular part of his work:

> Meetings start with a multicultural budget—a niche market. But then the numbers come back in and companies like Bud Light are doing business in supermarkets where they didn't have business before. Now, I'm saying: It's *total* market. Those num-bers helped me start to create the empire. Those numbers allow me to teach people and show them how to move the needle.

Because people are dancing to the music and smiling at the ads, they often don't see the full impact of what Pitbull is doing. But think about it this way. When dancers on a club floor in Lagos or Shanghai hear Pitbull's music, they swallow the Spanish and English lyrics and think of it as *American* music. The world hears Pitbull and thinks: That's *America*.

Contained in the pulse of the music is also a big clue to why Pitbull keeps upping the ante in everything that he does, refusing to set limits for himself, and urging others to do the same. Where does that drive come from? He says it has to do with the fact that "Latinos appreciate what it is to be free in this country and to be able to take advantage of opportunities and control your own destiny. So when you come with that kind of hunger it's real tough to not *eat* opportunity." By that, he means that when you see a goal that seems out of reach, "you say, 'What you mean I can't do that?' Of course I can and I just do it."

And so while you're watching him ring in the New Year or seeing headlines with his name and the words "billion-dollar brand," look closely and you will see the trajectory that has been leading us to the new sound of America.

CHAPTER THIRTEEN

From Mexico to Macy's

People think of Latina women as being fiery and fierce, which is usually true. But I think the quality that so many Latinas possess is strength. I'm very proud to have Latin blood.

—ZOE SALDANA

Many times in life you never really grasp the magnitude of what you are going through until you are no longer in the midst of it. Or at least that's what I realized in the years after I left Sony—where I had run the music division for a fifteen-, almost sixteen-year period. So it wasn't until 2004 and '05, as I stepped away and started to look back, that I really began to weigh the impact of the Latin Explosion, along with everything else that we as a company had generated in that time. All of it had taken place during what I believe will stand as the greatest period in music history.

Not that earlier periods weren't great. They were obviously the foundation for what came to fruition. That's why I feel so enormously blessed to have been part of building an empire of music that could never be created again. Out of that time at one company came more music icons than from any other; these are music legends who can be recognized by their first names alone and who would last on the global stage always—Bruce, Billy, Bob, Barbra, Céline, Michael, Mariah, Beyoncé, Gloria, Ricky, J. Lo, Marc, Shakira, and so on. Nowhere else had anything of that magnitude happened, nor would it again.

And what we were able to do to make that possible happened because it was a time when the opportunity was there, when we could. We seized the moment, and we did it. We did it on a world stage like it was never done before. At one point, someone at Sony told me in that period we sold 8 billion units—which represented 65 billion dollars of business. Four of the artists, all Latino, had in a matter of a few years sold 200 million dollars' worth of albums.

In hindsight, that seems so surreal. When you're in it, you don't think on that scale. You are in the trenches, like being at war, and you have to be a kind of infantry soldier—so that every day you go to battle. I never thought about what was happening as on that massive of a scale. When I did finally assess it all, my reaction was along the lines of, *"Holy shit, wow!"*

As I processed all of that and began to focus on new horizons, both in the entertainment business and in other marketing arenas, I became really passionate about sharing what I'd learned from the Latin Explosion. The passing of Celia Cruz on July 16, 2003, was an event that I kept thinking about—how her legacy was larger than the music itself.

In her seventy-seven years of life, Celia had recorded roughly seventy albums—the last one still to be released when cancer took her. Her body was flown to Miami for a special public viewing, and up to half a million people showed up in the summer heat to see her off in a line that stretched for at least fifteen blocks to Freedom Tower, the landmark Spanish Revival building that was once the Ellis Island for Cuban refugees.

Fans wept, tossed flowers and sugar at the hearse bearing Celia's casket, and shouted *"Azúcar!"* as it passed. A day later, her body was flown back to New York, where it was carried on a carriage drawn by two white horses down Fifth Avenue to a service at St. Patrick's Cathedral. La India, Jon Secada, Paquito D'Rivera, Johnny Pacheco, Rubén Blades, and so many other musicians whom Celia influenced were there to pay tribute.

There was really no need for an obituary. The words on the last track of her last album—a remake of the hit "I Will Survive"—said it all: *"In the soul of my people, in the skin of the drums, in the hands of the conga player, in the feet of the dancer, I will live on."*

Her passing made me want to do more to explore the legacy of other Latinos whose accomplishments in areas other than music mattered to American culture. Many of those I have touched on in earlier chapters. Probably the one area that I knew the least about in terms of the Latino influence was fashion and design. But that would change quickly.

When my wife, Thalia, was young and living in Mexico, getting a gift bag from Macy's was more than a gift. It was an announcement, a symbol.

Wow! You just got back from America . . .

Macy's was the first stop to shop for vacationers from Mexico and Latin America. It's only natural that back then, when Thalia opened a present coming out of a Macy's bag, she expected something special and different than what she'd normally find shopping at home.

And so it wasn't until many years later that she realized that Macy's did *not* have a devoted brand for Latinos.

It's always been kind of surprising to me that Latino influence in the fashion industry didn't move as rapidly into mainstream America as it did through music, food, and sports. I really don't see why it should've lagged behind, because Latinos have a pretty good track record when it comes to bold flair in all elements of design and style. Think about it. If this country was really so resistant to the Spanish language, then why has it been fashionable for so long for automakers to sell their cars by giving them Spanish names?

Needless to say, I know cars and I know that list goes on and on. Granada. Baja. Cordoba. Fuego. Sierra. Bronco. Fiesta. Tiburon. Santa Fe. Maxima. Hombre. El Camino. Eldorado. The names conjure an aura of style. No question.

Ironically, for anyone who can remember the Chrysler commercials that Ricardo Montalban, the height in class, would do dressed impeccably in a tuxedo and praising the virtues of "rich Corinthian leather," it turns out there is no such thing as Corinthian leather. The phrase was invented by an advertising firm. Apparently, a lot of the material used in the seat coverings of those Chryslers came from a supplier outside Newark, New Jersey.

Which tells you those advertisers knew what they were doing.

Because *just looking* at Ricardo in that ad made you want to sit behind the wheel of that car. Bold flair is a magnet and elegance will never go out of style.

There can be no denying the extraordinary talent of Latino designers. It's just that for the most part over the last sixty years the biggest splashes made by Latinos in the world of fashion have not landed in mainstream USA. They've been extremely high-end. And I'm not talking about Corinthian leather. I'm talking about the real deal—designers like Oscar de la Renta, Manolo Blahnik, Narciso Rodriguez, and Carolina Herrera.

The Dominican-born de la Renta dressed America's First Ladies for decades, starting in the sixties with Jacqueline Kennedy. The First Lady wanted to showcase only American designers, so her aides would sew the labels of a homegrown designer into outfits made by de la Renta—who was working out of Paris at the time. Nancy Reagan had no problem posing next to de la Renta in his work—especially when she was wearing dresses he made for her in her favorite color, red. Laura Bush celebrated George Bush's second inauguration in a white de la Renta gown. And Hillary Clinton once claimed that de la Renta had been working for twenty years "to turn her into a fashion icon."

Blahnik created a high-end shoe empire after watching his mother learn to make her own shoes from a cobbler in the Canary Islands. To this day Manolo crafts his designs with the care of a jeweler working on precious stones. The prices of Blahnik's shoes are way above the budget of an average buyer. But Blahnik's influence has been felt by a lot of people who've never stepped near his store in Beverly Hills. Back in the seventies, the designer was responsible for pointing the rest of the industry to the rescue of the sleek and sexy stiletto heel from the clutches of clunky platforms.

Rodriguez, the eldest child of Cuban parents, was put on the map when he dressed Carolyn Bessette for her wedding to John F. Kennedy Jr. And Carolina Herrera, from Venezuela, was asked by Jacqueline Kennedy Onassis to design the dress for her daughter Caroline's wedding.

With all this talent and fame, Thalia and I found it hard to believe how underrepresented Latino style has been in the mainstream. That was even after Latina stars like Jennifer Lopez and Eva Longoria attracted women of all ethnicities to the cosmetics and products they endorsed. The numbers make the argument: sales of CoverGirl's LashBlast mascara recently shot up 70 percent after Sofía Vergara became its ambassador.

And yet there was no Latino presence in the women's department of the largest and best department store in America, known for throwing the Thanksgiving Day Parade: Macy's.

The more Thalia and I looked into this white space, the more we discovered that there was virtually no upscale product serving the Latino customer anywhere at a mainstream price. The more we talked about it, the more we saw an opening for Thalia to create her own clothing line. Our friend Tommy Hilfiger understood the potential straightaway for an alliance with Macy's.

It was the perfect opening and the perfect match at just the right time. Macy's is a 28-billion-dollar company with 840 stores. Soon 20 percent of its customers are going to be Latino. There's no getting around that statistic for almost any retailer. Or the fact that Latino buyers are spending 20 percent more than non-Latinos, and they're spending more on fashion than other ethnic groups.

As we got to know Terry Lundgren, the CEO of Macy's, and moved forward, I saw how all the elements that created, touched, and sprang from the Latin Explosion would come together to help make the line a success. The expansive reach of Latin television. Social media and personal entrepreneurship. The growing Latino market in America. But Macy's added a vital new component, one that will be a game changer going forward.

For years, Latinos had to learn how to adapt to the United States. Now a pillar of American business was recognizing the importance of the emerging Latino market, the need to study it, and the need to adapt *to it*. This was not about putting a fiery or rugged name on a car for show, or getting a handsome actor in a tuxedo to persuade you to step inside. This was about truly understanding what genuinely worked best for Latinos and how that might cross over to the general population.

Thalia recalled the focus of our earlier conversations at Macy's:

I told them: Look, our culture is loyal. It's loving. It has family values. We're hard workers. But on top of that, we love to enjoy life. We love to have parties, to dance, to eat. If you translate those words into fashion, you have a home run. What do I mean by that? Well, if I eat some tortas on the Cinco de Mayo weekend, then I'm going to expand, and I need clothes that breathe with me, but yet make me look slim at the same time. The entire

Macy's design team took a trip to Mexico. They sat in malls to watch the way people walked. They took pictures of mothers and daughters. They studied textures and colors. They were meticulous; they're like an army. They did all the research that had never been done for this community.

This was respect. As the teams returned with their analysis on colors, styles, and fit, I had a sense that we were coming to the end of an era when major beverage companies would roll out commercials with bottles dressed as mariachis playing guitars and dancing on-screen. In the future, Latinos will no longer have to look at a commercial and wonder: *What do these gringos think, we just got off the banana boat?* Because companies like Macy's will be doing the research. And Latinos and Latinas will be included in the process of creating the commercials—and overseeing them.

With Thalia's guidance, and her taste for animal prints and gold trim, the team put together the smartest collection around, a collection that allowed Macy's to sell dresses, shoes, and even some entire outfits for less than one hundred dollars.

However, as Thalia pointed out, "The designs and colors were not the most important thing. The most important thing was the fit. They had to understand the curves of the Latina body. Once you get that right, you'll have a loyal client coming again and again and again."

As a singer and telenovela star, she understood why that was important, because as Thalia said, "Once a universal audience sees what a hit that is, that's when it will cross over."

We timed the launch to Thalia's performance on Univision's award show *Premio Lo Nuestro.*

The year and a half that we took to develop the line was a very rewarding time for me, again, because of everything I'd learned through selling music and turning unknowns into global superstars, combined with all the technological advances that had come after the Latin Explosion. We had those resources at our disposal to create a monumental brand.

It was such a different starting point from, say, when Gloria and Emilio Estefan had had to scrap and fight in the early eighties simply to make people understand who they were and what kind of music they were about. There was no waiting in lobbies. I believe that's a metaphor for where things are headed. Latinos are no longer starting from the bottom, and now they can get to the presidential suite.

In this case, Macy's was building on everything Thalia had accomplished throughout her career. She's been singing since age nine and has sold more than forty million records worldwide. Her telenovelas had played in 132 countries to billions of people and gotten number one ratings on Univision throughout fifteen years. And she had accumulated fifteen million Twitter followers along the way to a star on the Hollywood Walk of Fame. It made perfect sense for her star to shine alongside the big bright *red* star at Macy's. It was the perfect setup for everything to galvanize in a laser-sharp direction.

Macy's came through on its end with the biggest private-brand launch in the history of the company. We struck a major advertising deal with Univision that enabled Thalia to make appearances on the network's highest-rated television shows every day of the week during the launch of the Thalia Sodi Collection. We also created commercials in English and Spanish with a multicultural cast that turned the fitting room into a party. While at the same time seeking out the Latino consumer in every metro market.

The support and reach that Thalia had from the start from Macy's would have been unthinkable when I was getting my feet wet in the music industry. This was yet another reminder of the shifting grounds that will be propelling the next generation of entrepreneurial Latinos—because of the community that has been empowered to support fellow entrepreneurs.

Demographics and spending habits don't lie. One point five trillion in spending power showed its potency with the numbers that came surging through the doors. Our launch was so successful that in the first month we were 127 percent above projections in sales. And this was while a lot of other major brands were *down* double digits. At this writing, the Thalia Sodi Collection has become Macy's number-one-selling brand nationally. And international deals are beginning to be struck everywhere. It's evidence of the tremendous surge that Latinos are going to get when they can build opportunities and success from a position of leverage and power.

Not only that, but Latino successes like this one will lead to further successes. As the awareness of Thalia's line spreads, it only bodes well for upcoming Latina designers and products. The potency of the Latina market, by the way, is so significant that Coca-Cola has partnered with Cuban-born media entrepreneur Nely Galán to galvanize Latinas in a movement called Adelante. Galán, the former head and first female president of the television network Telemundo, and the creator of the reality show *The Swan*, encourages Latinas to own more businesses and to be consumers of products and services from businesses owned and run by other Latinas.

This is definitely a message whose time has come. It applies to all generations but none more so than those in the demographic of the young Modern Independent Achiever of today who has followed in the footsteps of Selena, the Tejano singer whose real dream was to leave her mark in fashion. Surveys show that the majority of today's MIAs believe that their daughters will have more financial stability, have more opportunities, and attain higher levels of education than they did.

Thalia would be the first to say that it was Selena who inspired her to see what could be possible—as a singer, actress, and now fashion entrepreneur. And it's no longer a matter of having to cross over to find assimilation and acceptance. American culture has made the crossover, really, rising up to take in the richness of the contributions being made.

The resounding success of Thalia's line at America's best department store made it clear to me that there are fewer and fewer places where Latin culture does not play a role in American space. Which leads us to the most important space of all.

CHAPTER FOURTEEN

The Latino Vote

McCain got 31 percent of the Hispanic vote in 2008. Romney got 27 percent in 2012. That's a downward trend that the Republicans really have to fix. There's a new rule in politics. No one really can make it to the White House without that Hispanic vote. No one can make it to the White House without Univision. They have to talk to us to get to the White House.

—JORGE RAMOS,
UNIVISION ANCHOR

Politics: the last frontier.

We can talk about the growing Latino population and predict the effect those numbers are going to have on America. We can bring up the new clout that will come with trillions of dollars of financial leverage. We can read books and watch documentaries about Latinos reinvigorating the culture through music, sports, and fashion. But only when huge numbers of Latinos step into the voting booths and elect the people they truly want to represent them will we witness the fulfillment of the promise of equality and opportunity for all.

To give you a sense of the political changes that have been taking place in the last quarter of a century, I have to share insights from a Robert Rodriguez movie called *Bedhead*.

It's a very short film—about nine minutes long—that Rodri-guez put together when he was getting started. It stars his younger sisters and brother. The main character is a typical Mexican-American girl whose daily life is made miserable in all the usual ways by an older brother. When her brother destroys her last doll, she can no longer contain herself and she charges at him.

In the tussle, she's flipped, her head smashes on concrete, and the collision gives her telekinetic powers. When she wants her brother's head to slam into a pole, for instance, all she has to do is wish for it, and like in a comic book he magically goes hurling into a pole without her having to lift a finger. When she suddenly real-izes she now has superhuman powers to do anything, she says: "I can even become the first Mexican-American female president of the United States!"

Audiences burst into cheers when they heard that line. Many of the viewers had never had or even considered a thought like that before in their lives.

It's easy to see why. For 225 years of American history, up until the movie *Bedhead* was released in 1991, there had only been five Latinos elected into the United States Senate. Since *Bedhead*, there have been six.

Up until *Bedhead*, there had been only twenty-eight Latinos voted into the House of Representatives. Since *Bedhead*, there have been forty-five.

You get my point here. Before Latinos can get to the White House, they have to put it on the line for themselves.

This brings me almost full circle to the question that really got me going on the HBO documentary and on this book—the question my daughter asked me on the night in November 2012, as we watched the returns of the presidential election coming in and heard one analyst after the next say that it would come down to the Latino vote.

What exactly did that mean? I began with more questions than answers.

One of the issues that comes up a lot when you talk about the strength of a voting bloc that is as culturally diverse as Latinos are in this country is the fact that they are by no means a monolithic group filled with predictable demographical thinkers who all vote alike. Yes, the majority of Mexican-Americans tend to vote for Democrats, and an even higher percentage of Puerto Rican–Americans aligns with the Democratic Party, as do the majority of Latino-Americans from Central and South America. Although the trends have changed in the last decade, more Cuban-Americans vote Republican than Democratic. Within all these leanings, about a third of Latinos see themselves as liberal, and another third see themselves as conservative, while slightly more than a third think of themselves as moderate.

Overall, if this would lead you to conclude that Democrats would benefit from these numbers during presidential elections, you would be right. In fact, going back to 1980, every single Democratic candidate for president has received more votes from Latino voters than the Republican candidate has. What has made the difference has been the margin.

In 1980, Jimmy Carter received 56 percent of the Latino vote, beating Ronald Reagan by 21 points. But that wasn't enough to give Carter the edge. In 'eighty-four Mondale won 61 percent of the Latino vote, pushing the margin to 24 points, but Reagan of course won his second term. Dukakis did even better in 'eighty-eight by receiving 69 percent of the Latino vote against George Herbert Walker Bush's 30 percent (a margin of 39 points). But in that year, other dynamics were in play and Latinos did not deliver the White House to the Democrat. In 1992, however, when Democrat Bill Clinton won the Latino vote by a margin of 36 points, that was enough to defeat Bush I, who only received 25 percent of the Latino vote. In 1996, President Clinton was reelected with 72 percent of Latinos' support—an advantage of 51 points over Bob Dole.

In the presidential election of 2000, Republicans were paying attention. Interestingly enough, their awareness happened at the same time that the Latin Explosion in music was really exploding. Taking nothing for granted, George W. Bush's campaign reached out to Latinos with a slogan of *Viva Bush!* His brand of compassionate conservatism, along with his stated goals of long-overdue immigration reform, was enough to give him 35 percent of the Latino vote. It wasn't enough to beat Vice President Al Gore in the popular vote. But in the electoral college, when it came down to Florida, Bush received considerable assistance from energized Latinos, mainly Cuban-Americans. Even though the determination was that Bush had won Florida by little more than five hundred votes, after an actual recount was stopped by the United States Supreme Court, the bottom line is this: Without the Latinos that did vote, there would never have been a Bush II in the White House.

Univision's Jorge Ramos put it into context by noting, "You can say whatever you want about President George W. Bush, but he did get the importance of the Hispanic community. If you go back to interviews with him, he tried to speak Spanish. People really appreciated the fact that he made an effort." Against John Kerry, President Bush took 40 percent of the Latino vote, a decisive edge in his reelection.

Awareness of the Latino vote ramped up considerably as Bush's second term began to tick down. The landscape was different. For some Latinos who had supported Bush, there were many reasons to throw their support in a new direction, especially after seeing no progress on immigration reform—and a President Bush who had promised to spend his political capital that he won by being reelected.

The first big news for Latinos came with the announcement that Bill Richardson, the Latino Democrat and governor of New Mexico, was running for president. Then a little-known exchange between Richardson and Barack Obama during a debate set up a critical swing.

The moment was fueled by the frustration Richardson felt as the campaign progressed. For years Latinos had been isolated in the political process, and Richardson believed that debate moderators were overlooking him while they focused on the front-runners—Hillary Clinton and Obama.

For some reason, or maybe it was simply coincidence, Obama and Richardson were positioned side by side during many of the debates, and they developed a rapport. They'd banter back and forth off camera in hushed tones that were inaudible to anyone else while other candidates were speaking on the opposite end of the stage.

When the very first question during this particular debate was posed to Richardson, he was happily surprised, and after he answered it he turned to Obama and joked that he might not get another chance to speak for the rest of the night. But his comment was ill-timed because just then one of the moderators immediately doubled back to him with another question, and Richardson didn't catch it. He was about to make the embarrassing concession of asking for the question to be repeated—a no-no—when a muffled voice came to his aid.

"Katrina," Obama whispered from behind a hand that he'd cupped over his mouth. "They asked you about Katrina."

Richardson got it together and nailed his answer, focusing on crisis management of future hurricanes. Then, as the debate moved on, he whispered, "Thanks, Obama. You're okay."

"Nothing to it, brother," Obama responded.

When Richardson bowed out of the 2008 campaign, he gave Obama his endorsement and a bloc of Latino support that came with it. That moment spoke loudly to many Latinos and gave them the same assurance that he was there to help.

Obama also reached out to the Estefans, Ricky Martin, Eva Longoria, and Pitbull. He had complete comprehension of Univision's enormous reach. And he knew that a very deep problem needed to be overcome. Latinos didn't vote—at least not in the numbers that they could amass.

Herein lies the challenge. Even today, this still holds true. Even with all their rising numbers and clout, Latinos don't vote at the rate that most Americans do. There are many understandable reasons for this. First of all, you've got to be older than eighteen to vote. And about 28 percent of Latinos are under eighteen. That's compared to 22 percent of non-Latinos. What's more, adults of voting age must be US citizens to vote. And only about 70 percent of Latinos are citizens—as opposed to 96 percent of non-Latinos. When those numbers are added up, just under 50 percent of Latinos are *eligible* to vote—as opposed to 74 percent of non-Latinos.

But of those eligible Latino voters, many simply don't go to the polls. It can be because of a language barrier, or because they're unfamiliar with or intimidated by the process—or because they just don't see how voting is useful to them.

Eva Longoria understands. Her perspective, as an activist who supports Democratic candidates, is:

> I've known so many Latinos who aren't apathetic; they just didn't understand how policy disproportionately affected their lives. A lot of the programs and outreach that the Democratic party has been doing is simply saying, "This is what happens when you don't vote." And then, "This is what can happen if you do vote."
>
> It's been amazing. I got to travel the country, talking to families and people about how policy affected their lives. You'd follow the stories. "I don't have health insurance because I lost my job and then this happened and now I don't have food

stamps." Or: "My daughter couldn't get into college because she didn't take the right courses when she was in high school and the public school didn't tell her . . ." All of these stories really humanize politics. The most important thing is to share those stories and share those experiences with the rest of the community, so people can go, "Wow, I didn't quite know that political decisions could affect you that way."

I think Latinos are starting to realize their political power. What Obama did was really awaken a sleeping giant within the Latino community, just by saying: "You matter. Your vote needs to be heard."

On Election Day in 2008, Latinos voted two to one for Obama and Joe Biden over John McCain and Sarah Palin. Obama-Biden took Florida with the Latino vote. They took California. They took New Jersey. But not only that. When they took New Mexico, the number of Latinos who voted jumped 9 percent. When they took Colorado, the number of Latino voters jumped 5 percent. And when they took Nevada, the number of Latinos who went to the polls jumped 5 percent.

The implications of a black man becoming the forty-fourth president of the United States were so huge that no single group could possibly take credit for it, and so many different people came together to celebrate. A quarter of a million people filled Grant Park in Chicago to hear Obama give his acceptance speech, and the crowd broke out in a refrain of "Yes, we can! Yes, we can!"

Any Latino who'd been around for a while knew it was an

adaptation of the slogan made famous by Cesar Chavez and Dolores Huerta back in the sixties:

Sí, se puede.

Being invited to the White House is always an honor, regardless of politics, especially for an immigrant or for anyone who has ever had to struggle for their right to belong. There's a great story recalled by Jaime Jarrín, the Dodgers baseball announcer in Spanish, about the time back in the 1980s when President Ronald Reagan met Mexico's president José López Portillo and Fernando Valenzuela was the most honored guest. Jarrín recalled:

> One of the greatest days I have had as an immigrant in this country was when I accompanied Fernando to the White House for that luncheon.
>
> When we were climbing the stairs to the dining room, I remember hearing these beautiful Mexican songs with great arrangements played by the Marine Corps Band. "Cielito Lindo." "Jalisco . . ."
>
> Just being in the White House is such a unique experience. But then came something else. After lunch, to see the most important people in the country, including President Reagan, George Bush, the vice president, Alexander Haig, the secretary of state, and Caspar Weinberger, the secretary of defense . . . all in line waiting for this nineteen-year-old kid who didn't speak English to sign them a baseball . . .

In the various administrations that followed, other milestones were reached as more and more Latinos achieved excellence in a growing number of fields and were honored for their contributions and their service.

Obama reached out to the Latino community as soon as he took office when he named two Latinos to his cabinet. The job of secretary of the interior went to a Mexican-American—the former governor of Colorado, Ken Salazar. While the position of secretary of labor was filled by the daughter of a Nicaraguan and a Mexican who'd met in a citizenship class—Hilda Solis.

But the president's most momentous move for Latinos came four months into his term, when he was faced with a vacancy in the Supreme Court. Filling a spot on the nation's highest court is one of the most important decisions a president can make because it's a lifetime appointment that usually outlasts even two presidential terms and can have ramifications for decades.

"No dream is beyond reach in the United States of America," Obama said, as he nominated Sonia Sotomayor for the seat. Sonia's mother wept as she watched, and for good reason.

Sonia's dad had only reached a third-grade education and had passed away when Sonia was nine, leaving her mother to work two jobs, at times, as she raised her children in a Bronx housing project. Sonia had no lawyers as role models. She didn't know any. Her path to Princeton and the *Yale Law Journal* started with Nancy Drew books.

When Sonia stepped to the podium to speak, she acknowledged

her mother through the theme of standing upon the shoulders of those who came before. "I am all I am because of her," she said, "and I am only half the woman she is."

Although Sonia had more experience at the time of her nomination than just about any other Supreme Court justice when he or she was appointed, and although she'd been appointed to positions during her ascent by both Democratic and Republican presidents, her nomination to the highest court in the land stunned a lot of people.

Jennifer Lopez shared her memory of watching the announcement of Sotomayor's Senate confirmation:

Marc and I were married at the time, and we were sitting in a hotel room watching the moment. My daughter, Emme, was there. My mom was there. And we were all just riveted, watching her achieve this thing that no Latina had ever achieved. All of us just had tears in our eyes.

Right away, we were like, "Wow! There's going to be a Latina president soon! It's going to happen, you know?" Later on, we had Sonia over for dinner to celebrate. She had been put through a lot of media scrutiny and she had to tough it out and deal with it, and she really came through. So we had this small, intimate dinner. Ricky Martin was there and a few other people.

I remember getting up and telling her, "You know why this was so important? It's inspiration. You became an inspiration for a generation of Latinos, and showed us all that there are no limits."

Marc Anthony put it this way:

In any walk of life, any occupation, you can find a prominent
Latino who's dominated a field at some point. There are more
and more of them. What bigger symbol of "anything is possible"
than these people? For the rest of my life, I won't be able to
say that there's never been a Puerto Rican Supreme Court justice. That's over. That feels good.

Not many months later, President Obama and the First Lady
went further in celebrating that forward progress by hosting an
event in the backyard of the White House, an unforgettable
experience for all of us who had the good fortune to be there. It was
called Fiesta Latina, and on the surface it was a night of music.
Gloria Estefan, José Feliciano, Marc Anthony, Los Lobos, and my
wife, Thalia, were among the special guests invited to sing.

The performances were tremendous. What an amazing moment
it was to watch when Thalia came down off the stage, walked to
the president's table and reached out her hand, and, of course,
President Obama got up on the dance floor to salsa with her. This
was much more than a party. The emotion in that tent told anyone
within it that Latinos would have their voices heard in the highest
places of the land from that moment on, and there was no better
symbol of that than when the entire audience stood to applaud the
newly appointed Supreme Court justice.

Nobody on earth could have been better than George Lopez

in that moment to poke just the right humor at the deep divide between some difficult days in the past and the elegant setting behind the White House.

"We'd like to thank you for having us over . . ." George said to the president. Then he paused at the irony. "Outside . . . in a tent . . . out back."

Then George turned to Supreme Court Justice Sotomayor. "I have to meet you officially," he cracked. "I got arrested and I wanted to make sure that if it gets to you we've made contact."

Underneath the laughter, you could feel every Latino and Latina in the room thinking back on his or her childhood as they took in their surroundings. "I've seen a lot of amazing things," George Lopez later quipped, "but Los Lobos with the White House in the back is one that I will never forget."

Another amazing moment that I only heard about took place at the Supreme Court after the end of Sonia Sotomayor's first term. Not only did Sonia have a stereo brought in to play salsa on it, but she promptly asked the other judges to join her on the dance floor.

And their reaction of laughter and enjoyment is the new sound of America.

We could all sort of see what was coming in 2012 as the election approached. We knew how the Latino vote had helped Obama win the presidency four years earlier. In the same month that he nominated Sotomayor, Julián Castro won an election to become the mayor of San Antonio. A mayoral win in a city that is more than 60 percent Latino may not seem very significant. Unless you see it as a springboard for all the subsequent moves on the political checkerboard.

The momentum of Obama's appointments and the Democratic advances in the Latino community had to be alarming to a lot of forward-thinking leaders in the Republican Party. They came back in the midterm elections by electing Susana Martinez as governor of New Mexico and Brian Sandoval as the first Latino governor of Nevada. Both are Republicans.

It was no surprise to me that the main keynote speakers at both 2012 political conventions were Latinos.

Florida senator Marco Rubio introduced Mitt Romney at the Republican convention with a call to the values of so many Latinos. Rubio, of Cuban descent, told the crowd: "We are special because we've been united not by a common race or ethnicity. We're bound together by common values. That family is the most important institution in society. That almighty God is the source of all we have."

Julián Castro, of Mexican descent, told the Democratic convention: "My grandmother never owned a house. She cleaned other people's houses so she could afford to rent her own. But she saw her daughter become the first in her family to graduate from college. And my mother fought hard for civil rights so that instead of a mop, I could hold this microphone."

Those paying particularly close attention, like Univision CEO Randy Falco and news anchor Jorge Ramos, saw how the Democrats were reaching out to the Latinos in a way that the Republicans just weren't.

Falco noted, "In the last election, President Obama came on Jorge's Sunday morning show, *Al Punto*, nine times. Governor Romney only came on one time. That shows you the difference in terms of a candidate who feels how important it is to actually talk to this community and the other candidate who, unfortunately for him, didn't."

Ramos went further, asserting, "There's a new rule in politics. No one really can make it to the White House without that Hispanic vote. No one can make it to the White House without Univision. They have to talk to us to get to the White House."

Barack Obama built on his ties to the Latino community in this second campaign, so much so that in 2012 his next labor secretary, Tom Perez, would go as far as to call Obama the first Latino president—much in the same way that the writer Toni Morrison referred to Bill Clinton as the first black president.

Sitting there as the vote was coming in, I knew that nothing was a slam dunk. But we all could see the map turning bluer and I figured something was really up when the Republicans lost the crucial state of Florida. *For the first time*, the generally conservative-leaning Cuban-Americans in Florida—now adding younger voters who were less mired in their parents' politics—voted for a Democratic candidate over a Republican.

Some would argue that Mitt Romney had lost the election with his "47 percent" comments, which painted him into a corner of elitism with lots of voting groups who might have been up for grabs.

His "binders full of women" comments had turned off, well, binders full of women's votes, for sure. It was just ironic that Romney couldn't find a way to connect to Latinos, despite the fact that his own father was born in Mexico.

And yet, Obama received 71 percent of the Latino vote and Romney only received 27 percent, less than any other presidential candidate for the last thirty-two years—other than Dole.

So how important are Latinos going to be as we move forward? Marc Anthony says it very plainly: "Politicians better pay attention. This is a constituency that you cannot ignore anymore. Ignore us at your own risk. This is not revolutionary talk in any way, shape, or form. This is about numbers." At the same time, Marc understands that in order for the numbers to matter, more Latinos need to register and vote. He goes on: "It's all about a basic grassroots education, educating Latinos in general about their rights and powers. You know, if you don't like the pothole in your street, you can talk to your councilman and ask him to do something about it. If the light doesn't work on the corner, you can get it fixed. You have a voice here. The power of this will be felt."

In reflecting on his own involvement and how to engage more Latino voters, Pitbull prefers to endorse the value of voting. He explains, "When Barack Obama came down to Miami, he asked me to go and speak. When I spoke, I gave him thanks, but I didn't tell anybody to vote for Barack Obama. Because what happens in politics, just as it does when it comes to brands and companies, is people try so hard to push them on you that you want to push them away. Better to let people make their own decisions. That's what I'm trying to teach. I'm not saying that you've got to do it one way or the other. I'm just saying, imagine if we used our clout, our power, our love, and our relationships to achieve the same goal . . . My God, it would be a tsunami, a megatsunami."

What is it that Latinos want to hear from their elected leaders?

For any candidate for office, that's a question worth answering. Cristina Saralegui says, "The common denominator all Latinos have is that we want some respect. That's what we're all fighting for."

Univision's CEO, Randy Falco, suggests that non-Latinos should learn more about Latino culture. He laughs and points out, "I tease my Republican friends and say that I think most Latinos are actually Republicans—they just don't know it. Latinos are very conservative. They're very religious, very family oriented. People just have to start to pay attention."

Julián Castro, who in 2014 went from mayor of San Antonio to become secretary of housing and urban development, offers these insights:

> I'm convinced that in order to get the Latino community to vote it's going to take more than just candidates or parties asking for their vote at election time. It's going to take a huge effort to make democratic participation relevant to their lives, whether it means the safety in their own neighborhood or the opportu-

nities that their children and grandchildren can have with a better education. Those types of things that reach the heart and soul of what they care about.

During the period just after Romney's defeat, the Republican National Committee and others attempted to do some serious soul-searching about how the party could do more to connect with minorities, women, and younger voters. Looking back, Romney admitted that his biggest strategic error was not investing sufficiently in advertising in outlets where Latino voters could understand the opportunities for them within the Republican Party.

Instead, it was Hillary Clinton who smartly moved into that space in 2014, as it happened, when Univision teamed up with the Clinton Foundation on a multiyear early-childhood initiative called Pequeños y Valiosos (Young and Valuable). So, in addition to the name association, there was Secretary Clinton's photo on the Univision website—at the same time that many voices within the Republican Party were taking hard-line stances against immigration reform.

Nonetheless, when the next presidential campaign season got under way, it was promising to see in the crowded Republican field that there were not one but two Latinos, both of Cuban descent, who had declared their candidacy—Senator Marco Rubio of Florida and Senator Ted Cruz of Texas. And then the candidate that many thought would be the one to beat was former Florida governor Jeb Bush, the son and brother to presidents, who speaks fluent Spanish, spent two years in Venezuela, and has a Mexican wife. Jeb once even mistakenly declared himself as Latino on a voter registration application.

No sooner had Donald Trump declared his candidacy for president, however, than his anti-immigrant and anti-Mexican rhetoric seemed to eclipse any positive outreach to Latinos that the RNC and the other candidates' campaigns might have undertaken. Trump's comments became the centerpiece for his campaign, which involved rounding up all undocumented Latinos, deporting them, and building a massive, "beautiful" wall along the border of the US and Mexico—with demands that the Mexican government pay for it.

Trump's rhetoric was highly inflammatory and offensive. The fact that he became the front-runner—and that his supporters backed these extreme positions—was deeply alarming. For many in the Latino community, this was seen as a backlash to the growing strength and presence of Latino citizens in America. But then something amazing happened in response.

Even though the hatred was being expressed toward Mexicans, and even though we know that Latinos make up many factions and communities who identify with their families' countries of origin, the racist rhetoric suddenly unified Latinos—who would answer in one voice.

That voice was to be in music. In September of 2015 *Billboard* magazine reported:

Grammy-winning producer Emilio Estefan has enlisted an all-star small army of famous friends—including Carlos Santana, Thalia, Pepe Aguilar, and his wife, singer Gloria Estefan—to combat the spate of anti-Mexican rhetoric that Donald Trump sparked earlier this summer.

Estefan, sixty-two, tells *Billboard* exclusively that, after listening to a TV talking head make false and vindictive anti-Latin statements on TV, he has rounded up dozens of Latin celebrities to record "We're All Mexican," which he describes as a musical "celebration of Hispanics and our accomplishments." The track, set to be released later in September, will also include reggaeton singer Wisin, radio personality Enrique Santos, and famed Spanish-American chef José Andrés, most of whom will be rapping on the record.

"There's a message being sent out to the world where people are giving opinions that are plain wrong," says the Cuban-American Estefan, who has won nineteen Grammy Awards. "We need to lift up our pride and show the world what we're doing."

Although issues of immigration and citizenship have long been lightning-rod topics of discussion among cable-news pundits, the public debate—on the airwaves and in the streets—has grown more brutish in the aftermath of comments made by Trump when he announced his presidential run in June. "When Mexico sends its people, they're not sending their best," Trump told an applauding crowd at the time. "They're sending people that have lots of problems, and they're bringing those problems [to] us. They're bringing drugs. They're bringing crime. They're rapists. And some, I assume, are good people."

Estefan, who says he's known Trump "for many, many years," insists that "We're All Mexican" "is not so much an answer to the real estate developer turned Republican candidate as it is an answer to the sentiment that we've progressed [as Hispanics] and we need to let people know that." And with this song, he adds, "I want to send a message that represents unity. Trump doesn't represent anything to me," Estefan tells *Billboard*. "Everyone has their opinion, and he can have whatever opinion he wants, as long as he doesn't humiliate my people."

It was right in character that Emilio and Gloria would create a song and a video for "We're All Mexican" in support of Mexicans and all Latinos, and in celebration of the American dream. As the project came together, more voices were added—those of Pitbull, Rita Moreno, Eva Longoria. And, of course, I was beyond proud to see Thalia right there with a smile and a sombrero.

Emilio had it right. Music was the best response.

When voter involvement increases, when Latinos are filling out ballots on school boards and local elections, when Latinos are arguing about Latino candidates on both sides of the spectrum, that's when we'll see the big change.

Latinos believe in the importance of public service and making a contribution to the country that has done so much for them and their families. Not enough can be said about the fact that Latinos have fought on behalf of this nation in far greater numbers than most of the general public knows—starting as early as the American Revolutionary War. In the Civil War, approximately 10,000 Mexican-Americans went into battle for both the North and the South. Incredibly, 200,000 Latinos fought in World War I and 500,000 Latinos served in World War II. Those numbers are remarkable, given the overall population of Latinos at the time. Hundreds of thousands more Latino-Americans would fight for their country over the next decades—in the Korean and Vietnam Wars, in our ongoing wars in Iraq and Afghanistan, and against terrorism. Latinos make up 18 percent of the Marines, the largest minority group to serve. Today, Latina women outnumber Latino men across the branches of the armed services.

Regardless of political party, one of the core values of Latinos as leaders is their patriotism. When you combine that with an entrepreneurial focus and an ability to solve problems, you are looking at the kinds of candidates for office that America needs and wants. But, again, it will happen when more Latinos vote in greater numbers.

And if Latinos confront political gridlock in their efforts, like the rest of us, well, maybe that's when we'll all know that Latinos are truly mainstream Americans. But I predict otherwise—that the sleeping giant of this amazing community has awakened and we'll celebrate a Latino in the White House in the not-too-distant future.

The trajectory of Latinos—unified and empowered—is not going to be stopped. Pitbull sees this arc as one that begins with economic empowerment. It's in the blood, the drive, the passion, the music.

He says it this way: "First we make the sandwiches. Then we own the restaurants. We clean the house. Then we own the houses. It's not the money. It's the journey . . . It's the fight."

This is the coming forth of his belief in "short steps, long vision." Pitbull lays down the gauntlet: "Next step, *La Casablanca. No hay carro, nos vamos en balsa.* Next step, the White House. If there's no car, we'll go by boat."

Meaning, one way or another, he says, "We'll get there."

CHAPTER FIFTEEN

The New Sound of America

America may not realize it yet, but Latin prototypes are being created right now, and not just by me. They are these mambo kings and salsa queens, Aztec lords and Inca princesses, every Hernandez and Fernandez, whom this country will one day come to understand and respect.

—JOHN LEGUIZAMO

Someone once said the best way of predicting the future is to create it.

No question. As we've seen all along, that is the essence of the story of Latinos and the seismic shift they created through their music, their culture, and their dreams. Nothing about where we are today should surprise us—now that the future has arrived and it has a new sound.

Such were my thoughts back in July 2014 when the entirety of Yankee Stadium was sold-out for not one but *two* consecutive nights to see bachata singer and pop superstar Romeo Santos. Out of nowhere, almost, it seemed that a Bronx-born singer of Dominican–Puerto Rican parentage had become one of the biggest Latino artists on the scene. In a fairly short time, bachata had gone from being a Dominican version of the blues, full of emotional songs about broken hearts and the bitter pain of love gone bad, to being an international music and dance phenomenon. And with Romeo Santos adding elements of hip-hop, pop, and R&B—including duets that he had recorded with everyone from Usher to Nicki Minaj and Marc Anthony—the once traditional bachata felt like it was on the cutting edge.

This was crazy. Caught up in the energy of the show, the massive crowd, mostly young, probably had no idea of the magnitude of the moment they were living.

But I knew.

I knew because I've been coming through the turnstiles at Yankee Stadium ever since I was a kid, and back then it was no place for a Latino to give a concert. Yankee Stadium back then was the home of the Yankees, and the site of the World Series, a heavyweight championship fight, or a visit from the Pope. Period.

Between his songs—and sets that featured fellow bachata heartthrob Prince Royce and a surprise appearance from icon Marc Anthony—Santos gave it up to his audience, as he always does, calling out to all the Latinos' different homelands. And the cheers that came back to him reverberated from every nook and cranny in the stadium. The Dominicans. The Puerto Ricans. The Mexicans. The Cubans. The Colombians. Salvadorans, Nicaraguans, Peruvians, Argentines . . . and so on. He doesn't like to leave anyone out. And at both of these two shows, he made sure he didn't.

Each night, Romeo Santos congratulated his fans, telling them,

"If Madonna, if Paul McCartney, if Metallica can sell out Yankee Stadium, Latinos can too!"

Somehow these two nights made it official to me. This was the future that had been created. Yankee Stadium was now truly the home of every Latino inside it as proudly as it was my own.

I thought a lot about what the reactions might have been back in the day if trailblazers who set the changes in motion could have been told where this was headed. Wow.

Think about the expression on Desi Arnaz's face if he could have been told at the height of *I Love Lucy* that in sixty years Latinos would be deciding the presidency. Or Rita Moreno. What if the moment she reached home safely as a girl after running from a white gang, she was told that in her lifetime she would see a day when studios would be looking for Latinos to fill out their films and mainstream advertisers would be looking for Latinos to endorse their products?

I wonder if it would have eased the struggle for a young Gloria Estefan—who remembers her mother looking for an apartment to rent in Miami and being met with signs that said, "No Pets, Children, or Cubans"—to have known that she, along with her husband, Emilio Estefan, would make an album of music honoring her homeland that would ignite a Latin Explosion. And how might all those musicians have felt knowing that because of their contributions, the value of their music would lead to a time when younger musicians and artists could bring their traditions into the future—and sell out Yankee Stadium?

And José Feliciano. What would he have said after he was briefly banished from the radio after his World Series performance in 1968 if he could have been told how his Christmas song sung in Spanish and English would make recording bilingual music a mainstay for a Latino known as Mr. Worldwide?

Come to think of it, I might even ask myself how my mother would have felt if she had known what she started when she danced with me on the streets of the Bronx to the music of Tito Puente.

All these musings aside, nobody could have predicted where we are today in the story that we've followed so far and that we'll continue to follow. It's a fact—the new sound of America has a Latino accent.

We went from the back-and-forth of Spanish and English on "Feliz Navidad" to radio jocks you now hear on stations in major cities casually speaking Spanglish. But wait.

Cut to: Facebook, where Spanglish is now certified as an official language.

That happened in roughly forty years. *Forty* years. It's all the more astounding when you look at this evolution through quick cuts. And it's even more inspiring now that you know how these changes unfolded step by step.

In 1950, one in fifty Americans was Latino. Blink your eyes. We've reached the point where it's soon going to be one in three Americans. In 2000 Latinos became the largest minority group. Ten years later, 45 million people in America speak Spanish.

Ricky Martin reacted to what has been the most significant demographic shift in US history by pointing out that the United

States is the second-largest Spanish-speaking country in the world. What do you say to that? What he did: "Boom!"

Sofía Vergara added her thoughts by saying, "We are everywhere, so, no matter what, you have to get used to us."

John Leguizamo, Puerto Rican–Colombian actor, comedian, producer, playwright, and screenwriter who narrated *The Latin Explosion*, the HBO documentary I produced as a partner to this book, explains how this evolution has happened. John says, "We are taking our culture and suturing it to America. Like gum on the bottom of a shoe, we are not going to disappear. Unlike other peoples who totally assimilated, we are more interested in co-assimilation."

He's right. And, as we've seen, as those influences were being absorbed, they've happened not only through music and entertainment, but in areas ranging from science to architecture to politics, as well as by the very basic values that a generation of Latina nannies is currently passing into mainstream America.

That's a point George Lopez makes when he notes, "So you have all of these little kids who are being taken care of by Latinas. They're doing a beautiful job. They're teaching these kids heart and soul and compassion, and love, every day. And you would never be taught that in a school. You could never be taught that in a college or at a university. So hands-on; wiping their faces, changing their diapers, picking them up when they fall, taking them to the park, changing their clothes, combing their hair, giving them baths: this all injects our culture into them."

The other half of the equation is that the new generation of

Latinos is changing too, as Latina marketer Monica Gadsby believes. Her stance is that the majority of kids today don't see color anymore. That's how her own Latino kids are growing up with what she calls "a new norm." Gadsby says, "It's just like they wouldn't know how to work a telephone with a rotary dial. It's not their fault, and it's not a big deal. They don't use their Latinness as a thing. They just are. We've gone from 'Honey, I'm home' to 'We're everywhere.'"

Echoing that reality, Cheech Marin asks, "So, what's a Georgia Chicano going to look like? What's a New Hampshire Chicano going to look like? An Alaskan Chicano. A Hawaiian Chicano. We're finding out. They take the best of both cultures and merge them."

The new sound of America is undoubtedly a multicultural one. Univision's Cristina agrees by saying this:

> My daughter is married to an Italian-American that she met in college in upstate New York. My two grandchildren are Italian-American. I would like, finally, all of us to get our act together. Instead of this competition and all this diffusion, that we get our act together. How you do that is through marriage and love and support. They are part of the pie—not separate anymore. My kids were born here. My grandkids have been born here. We're very proud not just of our roots, but of our country and what we, as a group, have added to the mix.

Cheech Marin talks about what the new mainstream in America is:

Last year, in this country, 50.6 percent of the children were Latino. That's the majority. And so every one of those kids is going to have a hundred kids apiece, 'cause that's how we roll. And it's happening in every state simultaneously. This is American culture. This is not separate from American culture.

When I address groups that are totally Latino, I say: I'm speaking to the mainstream here. People should start to recognize that this is the mainstream and it's going to just get bigger and bigger. It's a wonderful infusion of energy that this country needed. The payoff is a greater standard of living. More tolerance for everybody. The recognition that Spanish was the very first European language spoken in the United States, by a hundred years.

Chicago was the second-biggest conglomeration of Mexicans in the US—since the thirties. It's a silent thing. It's like the title of the book I'm working on called *We Come in Peace, but We Have You Surrounded.*

What will the next chapter in the journey look like?

Eva Longoria answers, "I think people have this fear that there's going to be a Taco Bell on every corner and the national language is going to change to Spanish. That's not what's going to happen. What's going to happen is we're just going to have this beautiful, amazing culture throughout the country, just like we have had historically with the arrival and emergence of other groups. There will be certain things and traditions that we still hold on to in this country that were born of another culture—just as there always have been. But my dream is that we won't really have to talk about Latino, or African-American, or white. That those descriptions become irrelevant, and we just evolve into a community of human beings."

Again, that's a future we can predict if we strive to create it. There may be passing signs of the times—hate, backlash, political scapegoating of Latinos as they become empowered at all levels— and those can be cause for concern. But what I know in my heart is that all that noise doesn't reflect the views of most Americans. What I also know is that when you rise above the noise with music, something transformational happens. If you add to that the other aspects of culture—humor, food, all forms of entertainment, voices in media and in literature, and then passion, a devotion to family and country, entrepreneurial vision, and leadership on every front—love wins.

Yes, this is a love story—one that began for me as a young boy with the Latino influences on the streets of the Bronx and grew as I met more and more talented Latino musicians while I was a manager and then when I took over at Sony Music, and ultimately led me to the love of my life and two wonderful young kids, who are now a symbol of where this country is headed.

The Latin Explosion was exactly the opportunity that spoke to someone as creatively obsessive, driven, and passionate as me. And even though the music industry has become a totally different business than it once was, forever and ever the music of Latinos, with its sexy, infectious, danceable rhythms, will matter to the ears of the world.

And Latinos themselves. If I can tell you one thing about my household whenever we have our multicultural family gatherings—including all of my four kids and the Italians and Jews and all the Mexicans from Thalia's side of the family—yes, the Latinos are the loudest.

They're loud. They don't know how to speak normally. Everything is on ten. The volume is always up. They are beautiful, passionate, colorfully animated, and they have something to say and you're going to listen. They walk into the room and you know it. What else can I say?

And so here's what that tells us.

If history is any measure, the best characteristics of every culture that comes to America merge with the best traits of all the cultures that have already called this country home, only to evolve into something new. We call it a new sound for America because shared culture is a celebration. Who doesn't want to be at this party?

Going forward, this evolution will contain the difficulties faced and successes accumulated by the recording artists and entertainers who appeared throughout this book, as well as the gritty rise of Latinos not necessarily in the spotlight but who have become the backbone, the very spine, of the United States workforce.

This evolution is about people who are worthy. Wonderful people who, yes, are full of color and full of life, and, once again, people who have something to say and who want to be heard and now who will be heard. Beautiful people who are making huge contributions, and doing so with gusto and tenacity. Proud people who love America, who are at one with this country, and who are making it their own.

Thank you for coming on this journey to look back at how we got here. I can't wait for where it's going next. Because in 2040, should my youngest children have children, they will be able to tell them how things turned out to be the way they are, because they'll also know a little more about the music and the culture that defined a period of time called the Latin Explosion, and how it touched everything that came to be and helped to create a new sound for America for all.

ACKNOWLEDGMENTS

I want to thank everyone who participated in this book, for it carries a message I feel so strongly about—a powerful statement about Latinos and the importance of music and the future of America.

A huge amount of research went into this book, and I deeply appreciate everyone who was part of the process, especially those who shared their personal journeys—which I'm sure will inspire and resonate with each and every reader.

Latinos and the United States of America have come a long way during the time period that frames this book. Many of the people below were instrumental in guiding us across that distance. We all owe them our thanks, as will the generations to come.

Marc Anthony

Lucie Arnaz

Chiqui Cartagena

Julián Castro

Charo

Alberto Dávila

Gloria and Emilio Estefan

Randy Falco

José Feliciano

Acknowledgments

Monica Gadsby

Nely Galán

Jacqueline Hernández

Jaime Jarrín

John Leguizamo

Eva Longoria

George Lopez

Jennifer Lopez

Cheech Marin

Ricky Martin

Luis Miguel Messianu

Rita Moreno

Arturo Nunez

Edward James Olmos

Pitbull

Jorge Ramos

Rico Rodriguez

Robert Rodriguez

Cristina Saralegui

Shakira

Thalia

Rafael Toro of Goya

Sofía Vergara